Treasure Boxes

Teacher's Guide

Grades K–3

Skills
Collecting, Observing, Comparing, Describing,
Measuring, Communicating, Organizing,
Experimenting, Recording, Drawing Conclusions,
Sorting, Classifying, Counting, Mapping, Graphing,
Computation, Number Sense, Problem Solving,
Logical Thinking

Concepts
Classification, Venn Diagrams, Graphs,
Coordinate Grids, Number, Division, Recycling,
Literature Connections to Math

Themes
Diversity and Unity, Matter, Patterns of Change,
Structure, Systems and Interactions

Mathematics Strands
Discrete Mathematics, Geometry, Logic and
Language, Pattern, Number, Measurement, Statistics

Nature of Science and Mathematics
Cooperative Efforts, Real-life Applications,
Interdisciplinary

Time
Six 30- to 60-minute activities

by
Jaine Kopp
with
Kimi Hosoume

LHS GEMS

Great Explorations in Math and Science
Lawrence Hall of Science
University of California at Berkeley

Cover Design	Illustrations	Photographs
Lisa Klofkorn	Lisa Klofkorn	Richard Hoyt
		Laurence Bradley

Lawrence Hall of Science, University of California, Berkeley, CA 94720-5200

Chairman: Glenn T. Seaborg
Director: Ian Carmichael

Initial support for the origination and publication of the GEMS series was provided by the A.W. Mellon Foundation and the Carnegie Corporation of New York. Under a grant from the National Science Foundation, GEMS Leader's Workshops have been held across the country. GEMS has also received support from: the McDonnell-Douglas Foundation and the McDonnell-Douglas Employee's Community Fund; the Hewlett Packard Company; the people at Chevron USA; Join Hands, the Health and Safety Educational Alliance; the Microscopy Society of America (MSA); and the Shell Oil Company Foundation. GEMS also gratefully acknowledges the contribution of word processing equipment from Apple Computer, Inc. This support does not imply responsibility for statements or views expressed in publications of the GEMS program. For further information on GEMS leadership opportunities, or to receive a catalog and the *GEMS Network News*, please contact GEMS at the address and phone number below. We also welcome letters to the *GEMS Network News*.

International Standard Book Number: 0-924886-64-1

COMMENTS WELCOME !

Great Explorations in Math and Science (GEMS) is an ongoing curriculum development project. GEMS guides are revised periodically, to incorporate teacher comments and new approaches. We welcome your criticisms, suggestions, helpful hints, and any anecdotes about your experience presenting GEMS activities. Your suggestions will be reviewed each time a GEMS guide is revised. Please send your comments to: GEMS Revisions, c/o Lawrence Hall of Science, University of California, Berkeley, CA 94720-5200. The phone number is (510) 642-7771. The fax number is (510) 643-0309.

Great Explorations in Math and Science (GEMS) Program

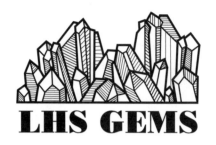

The Lawrence Hall of Science (LHS) is a public science center on the University of California at Berkeley campus. LHS offers a full program of activities for the public, including workshops and classes, exhibits, films, lectures, and special events. LHS is also a center for teacher education and curriculum research and development.

Over the years, LHS staff have developed a multitude of activities, assembly programs, classes, and interactive exhibits. These programs have proven to be successful at the Hall and should be useful to schools, other science centers, museums, and community groups. A number of these guided-discovery activities have been published under the Great Explorations in Math and Science (GEMS) title, after an extensive refinement and adaptation process that includes classroom testing of trial versions, modifications to ensure the use of easy-to-obtain materials, with carefully written and edited step-by-step instructions and background information to allow presentation by teachers without special background in mathematics or science.

Staff

Principal Investigator: Glenn T. Seaborg
Director: Jacqueline Barber
Associate Director: Kimi Hosoume
Associate Director/
Principal Editor: Lincoln Bergman
Science Curriculum Specialist: Cary Sneider
Mathematics Curriculum Specialist: Jaine Kopp
GEMS Network Director: Carolyn Willard
GEMS Workshop Coordinator: Laura Tucker
Staff Development Specialists: Lynn Barakos, Katharine Barrett, Kevin Beals, Ellen Blinderman, Beatrice Boffen, Gigi Dornfest, John Erickson, Stan Fukunaga, Philip Gonsalves, Cathy Larripa, Linda Lipner, Debra Sutter
Financial Assistant: Alice Olivier
Distribution Coordinator: Karen Milligan

Workshop Administrator: Terry Cort
Materials Manager: Vivian Tong
Distribution Representative: Felicia Roston
Shipping Assistants: Ben Arreguy, Bryan Burd
GEMS Marketing and Promotion Director: Gerri Ginsburg
Marketing Representative: Matthew Osborn
Senior Editor: Carl Babcock
Editor: Florence Stone
Principal Publications Coordinator: Kay Fairwell
Art Director: Lisa Haderlie Baker
Senior Artist: Lisa Klofkorn
Designers: Carol Bevilacqua, Rose Craig
Staff Assistants: Kasia Bukowinski, Larry Gates, Trina Huynh, Steve Lim, Jim Orosco, Christine Tong

Contributing Authors

Jacqueline Barber
Katharine Barrett
Kevin Beals
Lincoln Bergman
Beverly Braxton
Kevin Cuff
Linda De Lucchi
Gigi Dornfest

Jean Echols
John Erickson
Philip Gonsalves
Jan M. Goodman
Alan Gould
Catherine Halversen
Kimi Hosoume
Susan Jagoda

Jaine Kopp
Linda Lipner
Larry Malone
Cary I. Sneider
Craig Strang
Debra Sutter
Jennifer Meux White
Carolyn Willard

Reviewers

We would like to thank the following educators who reviewed, tested, or coordinated the reviewing of *this series* of GEMS materials in manuscript and draft form (including the GEMS guides *Treasure Boxes, Group Solutions, Tool!* and *Schoolyard Ecology*). Their critical comments and recommendations, based on classroom presentation of these activities nationwide, contributed significantly to these GEMS publications. Their particpation in the review process does not necessarily imply endorsement of the GEMS program or responsibility for statements or views expressed. This role is an invaluable one; feedback is carefully recorded and integrated as appropriate into the publications. **THANK YOU!**

CALIFORNIA
Jefferson Elementary School, Berkeley
Andrew Galperi
Jan Goodman
Barbara Hopkins
Linda Mengel
Maggie Riddle
*Fern Stroud
Beverly Thiele
Annie Tong

Malcolm X Intermediate School, Berkeley
Candyce Cannon
Carole Richardson
Louise Rosenkrantz
*Mahalia Ryba

Fairmont Elementary School, El Cerrito
Nanci Buckingham
Carrie Cook
Katy Miles
Nancy Rutter-Spriggs

Madera School, El Cerrito
Kristine J. Heydon
*Janet P. Johnson
Laurel Miller
Anne Paulsen
Sue Ellen Raby
Nancy Smythe

M. H. Stanley Intermediate School, Lafayette
Mark Brune
Glen Hoxie
Michael Merrick
Amy Wright

Multnomah Elementary School, Los Angeles
Sheryl Kampelman
Lucy Nigh
Elaine Peters
Connie Wright

Neil Hafley Elementary School, Manteca
Jill Durham
Lesley Fontanilla
Dorothy J. Land
Nina M. Winters

Park Day School, Oakland
Harriet Cohen
*Karen Corzan
Martina Kaumbulu
Michelle McAfee Krueger

St. Augustine School, Oakland
Diane Dias
Todd Jacobson
Monica Middlebrook
Pat Schmitz

Stonehurst Elementary School, Oakland
Harriet Axlerod
Christy Grierson
Irene Herring
Claudio Vargas

Grant Elementary School, Richmond
Terril Bertz
Kathy Clemons
Shelly Gupton
Mary Mallet
Pam Roay

Wilson Elementary School, San Leandro
Sally Barry
Jason Browning
Sarah Del Grande
Sue Reed Chevez
*Maggie Swartz-Nierlich

Downer Elementary School, San Pablo
Antonietta Franco
Lourdes Gonzales
Jennie Gragan
Grita Kamin
Eileen Malone
Galen Murphy
*Lina Jane Prairie
Marylee Stadler
Emily Vogler

CONNECTICUT
Allgrove School, East Granby
Tammy Chasse
Kathy Iwanicki
Kristi Smith
Patricia Smith

Plainfield Memorial School, Plainfield
Carol Bellavance
Laurie Brunsdon
Linda Gluck
*Lynne Terry

FLORIDA
Gulfstream Elementary School, Miami
Adrienne Cohen
Fran Cohen
Robert Martin
Angela Taylor

IDAHO
Washington Elementary School, Pocatello
Cathy Kratz
Tacia Tsakrios
Kathleen Wilike
Kristie Wolff

INDIANA
Lincoln School, Hammond
Linda McHie
Robin Miller
Tina Roznawski
Barbara Walczak

LOUISIANA
Alice M. Harte Elementary, New Orleans
Lynn Baker
Janice Catledge
Marilyn "Cookie" Vallette
Margaret Wells

MISSOURI
Blades Elementary School, Mehlville
Sherlee Garland
Susan Jesse
Rick Livesay
Lisa Madigan
Dawn Meyer
*Susan Steinkiste

NEVADA
Dayton Elementary School, Dayton
Gail Bushey
Stacy John
Kathy Newman
Karla Rodriguez

Winnemucca Grammar School, Winnemucca
Cheryl Bishop
Maria Crawford
Naomi Menesini
*Susan Putnam
Pilar Ramsdell

NEW MEXICO
Matheson Park School, Albuquerque
Gloria Archunde
Kris Donahue
Jayne Grant
Judith Gumble
Cynthia Themelis

NEW YORK
Public School 87, New York City
Miriam Ayeni
Leslie Corbin
Robert D'Andrea
Betty Lerner

NORTH CAROLINA
Haw Creek Elementary School, Asheville
Sandra Duckett
Donna Edmiston
Sue Jensen
Marta Johnson

NORTH DAKOTA
Dakota Elementary School, Minot AFB
*Apryl M. Davenport
Linda Dickerson
Sherry Heilmann
Vicki Summerfield

SOUTH CAROLINA
Bryson Elementary, Simpsonville
Marsha Basanda
Melanie S. Helling
Lisa T. Hoffman
Linda Jennings

TEXAS
Harry C. Withers Elementary School, Dallas
*Natala Assa
Sarah Jones
Liz Luester
Alex Rodriguez

Tom C. Gooch Elementary School, Dallas
Janie Broadnax
Flavia Burton
Harry Deihl
Kara Johnson
Tanda Pohl
Bill Wooley

* On-Site Trial Test Coordinator for *Treasure Boxes*

Acknowledgments

For many, first mention of "treasures" evokes visions of treasure chests filled with diamonds, rubies, gold, silver, and/or lots of money! These are certainly material treasures, but they do not represent the most valuable treasures in life. Family and friends, beautiful natural places, a hand-crafted gift, an heirloom passed down through generations of time—these are the true treasures of the heart and spirit.

In that light, I would like to thank and acknowledge my family for all their support in the many forms it has taken over the years. Each of you has helped me to reach the place where I am today. I love and treasure every one of you. Alan and Chenoa...special thanks to each of you for your extra support as this work came to fruition.

Sometimes we are lucky enough to have colleagues who are also dear friends. Kimi Hosoume, GEMS Associate Director, is one of those treasures in my life. In the writing of this guide, Kimi served as my "GEMS buddy" and provided invaluable support and insight as these activities were tested, written, revised, and transformed into their final form. Kimi's high standards and attention to detail helped make this "GEM" shine.

Though I have presented diverse versions of these activities over many years of teaching, this guide would not have come into being without the active encouragement of Jacqueline Barber, GEMS Director. I want to thank Jacquey for sharing her love of treasure activities and for having the vision to see the unit's full potential.

The initial seeds for this guide were planted by the work of Mary Barrata Lorton, whose book, *Mathematics Their Way*, written in the early 1970s, revolutionized math education. Through her work I was introduced to "junk" boxes—further developed and transformed into this unit's "treasure boxes."

Lina Jane Prairie of Downer Elementary School in San Pablo, California, a dedicated teacher who seeks to ensure that all children in her class learn and succeed, opened her classroom of lively second graders for local pilot testing of these activities. Her enthusiastic second graders spurred the activities on with their interest in and excitement about treasures and mathematical adventures. Thank you all!

Special thanks also goes to Sally Barry, Jason Browning, Sarah Del Grande, and Maggie Swartz, outstanding teachers at Wilson Elementary School in San Leandro, California, for trial testing these activities and for the generous gift of their time in allowing us to photograph the *Treasure Boxes* activities in their classrooms. And, of course, many thanks to the students whose bright faces grace the photographs that enliven this guide.

Children are truly our treasures…

Contents

Calvin and Hobbes

by Bill Watterson

Introduction

Treasure Boxes is an engaging unit in which students use collections of small, interesting objects in an innovative series of mathematics activities. Working with these "treasures" provides fresh and exciting ways for your students to learn and grow. Many important skills as well as science and mathematics concepts come to life.

Such collections of small objects, known by many names other than treasures, have often been used in mathematics programs. *Treasure Boxes* synthesizes this body of previous experience to create a new and original sequence of activities that build upon each other, in order to draw out the greatest possible educational richness from the "treasures."

Motivated by the appeal of the treasure boxes, your students actively observe, compare, describe, organize, communicate, record, and draw conclusions. On the way, they develop skills and abilities that will truly serve them as "valuable treasures" as they approach all their future learning. In addition, your students work through each activity cooperatively and collaboratively.

The mathematical content of this unit is rich. Through sorting, making Venn diagrams, and graphing, students work in age-appropriate areas of statistics, discrete mathematics, logic, language, and number—areas of mathematics recommended in the *Curriculum and Evaluation Standards for Teaching Mathematics* by the National Council of Teachers of Mathematics (NCTM). In the Hidden Treasure Map game, students gain experience with a coordinate grid that helps prepare them for coordinate geometry and advanced graphing. Computational skills are also reinforced as they divide cereal and treasures. Multiple solutions to questions and problems encourage student understanding of different strategies and approaches to problem solving, also called divergent thinking skills.

Activities Building On Each Other

Activity 1: Collecting Treasures serves as the foundation for the unit, as your students participate in creating the collections of treasures. This adds to the educational power of the treasures. When students help collect the treasures, they have pride in and develop a strong connection to the collections. The treasures can include "recycled" items (such as bottle caps, buttons,

For those of you who may be "pack rats," here is one way to put that collection of odds and ends to good use. And for those of you new to collecting, fear not! Spurred on by their enthusiasm for treasures, your students will help fill the boxes in no time at all!

canceled stamps, and keys), "found" items (such as rocks, seed pods, and shells), or inexpensively purchased items (such as pasta or plastic toy animals). Using recycled materials is a great way to find new value in throw-away items and to reinforce the importance of recycling and reuse in caring for the environment. Each box needs about 30–36 items for it to serve as an effective teaching tool.

Activity 2: Exploring Treasures strongly emphasizes free exploration. Your students make their own discoveries as they freely explore the treasure boxes they have filled. As they make discoveries about the attributes of the treasures, their curiosity is stimulated further, which in turn leads to more exploration. One of the best things about free exploration is that everyone is successful—there are no "right" or "wrong" answers! This activity also sets the stage for more directed activities.

Activity 3: Treasures of Many Sorts focuses on attributes and sorting. Using language and logical thinking skills, students identify attributes of the treasures and sort a box of treasures in a variety of ways. The high interest in and strong connection to treasures makes these materials simply superb for the natural development of sorting and classifying abilities. Second and third grade students are introduced to Venn diagrams and challenged to organize their treasures with this important mathematical and logical tool.

Activity 4: Treasure Graphs builds on student knowledge from the previous sorting activity to strengthen graphing abilities and introduce students to useful ways to summarize and visualize data. In this activity, your students organize treasures on graphing grids. As they observe how the treasures are organized, they make "true statements" about the data on the graphs. This concrete experience with statistics provides a solid foundation for students to interpret data they encounter in real world settings.

Activity 5: Treasure Maps features an involving game to branch out into new mathematical areas. Using a coordinate grid that serves as the "Treasure Map," students have fun finding treasures "hidden" on the map. The students play two versions of a treasure map game— one to become familiar with the grid and the other to guess coordinates. Playing the game gives them valuable practice with a coordinate grid and reinforces map reading skills.

Activity 6: Sharing Treasures brings cooperation and sharing to the fore while organically introducing division. In this final activity, students find ways to equally divide a group of items. In small groups, they begin by sharing a portion of cereal—each person has to participate and agree that the cereal has been divided fairly. Next, they divide treasures in several ways. This gives students an opportunity to see that the same quantity can be divided in more than one way and gives students concrete experience with division skills.

Taken together, these six main activities build upon one another to allow students to gain experience and develop their abilities in many areas of mathematics—and science as well. Careful observation, sorting and classification, logical thinking skills, graphing and other ways to analyze data—all of these interweave in both math and science and throughout this unit.

Opportunities for assessment are embedded throughout the activities and highlighted in the "Assessment Suggestions" section. Literature that supports these activities is frequently suggested and many excellent books are listed in "Literature Connections." The "Going Further" section provides ways to extend the initial activities—both for younger and older students.

We're sure you and your students will come up with many imaginative ways to connect these activities across the curriculum and to daily life. Most of all, delight in the treasures and enjoy watching your students learn! For they are the greatest treasures!

Time Frame

The first time you present this unit, you will create your initial treasure boxes with the help of your students. These boxes are a non-consumable material that will be a permanent classroom manipulative for both science and mathematics activities. The time involved to make them is built into the first activity. There are three other non-consumable materials that require an initial preparation time. The approximate times needed to make these items are included in this time frame. Once these items have been made, they can be used each time you teach *Treasure Boxes.* Many teachers use them for additional activities as well.

For all the activities, there is a minimal amount of time needed to gather the materials listed in each "What You Need" section. The time frames for doing the activities are broken into sessions and are estimated. Please be aware that times will vary depending upon your schedule, class size, and particular group of students. You know your students best and can adjust accordingly.

Activity 1: Collecting Treasures

    Session 1: Setting the Stage to Collect Treasures................30 minutes
    Session 2: Filling the Boxes with Treasures....................30–45 minutes

Activity 2: Exploring Treasures

    Classroom Activity...30–45 minutes
    Note: Students benefit from revisiting this activity several times before continuing with the following activities.

Activity 3: Treasures of Many Sorts

    Preparation...15–20 minutes
    Session 1: Shoe Sort..30 minutes
    Session 2: Sorting Treasures...30–45 minutes
    Session 3: Venn Diagrams to Sort Treasure.............45–60 minutes

Activity 4: Treasure Graphs

    Preparation...30 minutes
    Session 1: Graphing Shoes...30 minutes
    Session 2: Graphing Treasures...30–45 minutes

Activity 5: Treasure Maps

    Preparation...10 minutes
    Session 1: HiddenTreasure Hunt.............................30–45 minutes
    Session 2: Hidden Treasure Game............................30–45 minutes

Activity 6: Sharing Treasures

    Preparation...20 minutes
    Session 1: Cereal Sharing...30–45 minutes
    Session 2: Dividing Up Treasure!............................30–45 minutes

Activity 1: Collecting Treasures

Overview

One of the great beauties of treasure boxes is that your students help to create them. They contribute recycled items from their homes, the schoolyard, and even from field trips. Another great attribute of treasure boxes is that they are inexpensive—the major investment is in the small cardboard boxes that hold the treasures. Once the collections are made, students explore and use the treasures to investigate both science and mathematics concepts.

In Session 1, your students have about one week to collect and bring in materials. As a group, they share their treasures. You are likely to hear lots of "oohs" and "aahs" as they check out each other's collections. In Session 2, the boxes are labeled and an initial sorting of materials begins as the boxes are filled with their respective treasures. Throughout the year, additions can be made to these first treasure boxes and new boxes may be inspired by the contents of others.

This is a great activity to open the school year. The students are all involved and have a meaningful way to share with their classmates.

Students develop a great respect for and personal connection to treasure boxes as they create them. The process of sharing materials with one another helps to build a cooperative learning environment in the classroom. These collections also help students to see how to recycle and reuse materials in new and different ways.

Families are also involved in the treasure collecting. Through a letter that explains treasure boxes, families assist their children in acquiring materials. This provides an opportunity to talk about school activities at home.

What You Need

For the class:
- ❏ 32 copies of the Sample Letter to Families (master on page 89)
- ❏ 32 1 ½" x 1 ½" construction paper squares
- ❏ 8–16 sturdy empty boxes
- ❏ 1 permanent marker to label boxes
- ❏ extra treasures for students who may not have collected their own and to show to students as examples
- ❏ a few treasure items the same size, smaller, and larger than the construction paper square
- ❏ a few personal treasures to share with the class
- ❏ chart paper
- ❏ 1 large box for collecting all class treasures
- ❏ (*optional*) 32 sandwich size ziplock plastic bags

Getting Ready

1. Decide how many treasure boxes you want to have for your classroom. Depending upon the grade level of your students, the number of boxes is likely to vary. In kindergarten, students work best with only one partner, so it is good to start with one box per pair of students. Older students are more able to share these high interest materials; groups of four can share a box. It is also fine to have boxes that contain the same materials, such as two treasure boxes with bottle caps, especially if there is high interest in that material.

One teacher reported that her eye doctor was a great source for boxes. Another teacher used shoe boxes from young children's shoes. Though quite a bit larger, they are good for large collections or collections of larger items.

2. Decide what type of sturdy box you want to use. Business card boxes (size: 10 ¹⁄₁₆" long x 3 ⅝" wide x 2" deep) are particularly well-suited for treasure boxes. Many large stationery and paper supply stores sell them, or you could check with local businesses for donations of boxes. (Sources for business card boxes are listed on page 68.) Gather the quantity and type of box upon which you have decided.

3. Compose your own letter to parents and families that explains the *Treasure Boxes* unit, or duplicate the sample letter on page 89.

One teacher drew the square directly on the parent letter. Then when they're at home the students can cut out the square and use it as a measuring tool.

4. Cut enough construction paper squares to attach one to each letter that goes home to families.

5. Collect, and have on hand, additional treasures for those students who may not have been able to collect enough of their own and to show to students to give them an idea of the type of treasure they'll collect.

6. Gather a few items that are the *same size* as the construction paper square, *smaller* than the square, and *larger* than the square to demonstrate how to determine the size of objects that can fit into the treasure boxes.

7. Choose a few personal "treasures" that you want to share with the class. These might be a family keepsake, something that was hand-crafted for you, or a "souvenir" (shell, pine cone, rock) from a trip.

Some possible treasures to collect are buttons, shells, rocks, old keys, stamps, foreign coins, pasta in a variety of shapes, barrettes, paper clips, pencil erasers, puzzle pieces, nuts, bolts, and screws.

Session 1: Setting the Stage to Collect Treasures

1. Gather your students in an area away from their desks. Tell them that as a class they're beginning an exciting new project that involves making collections of small treasures. Begin by asking what a treasure means to them. Have everyone close their eyes and imagine treasures. It is likely that their initial concept of treasure will be materially valuable things such as money, precious metals, and jewels.

A treasure definition:
• accumulated or stored wealth—especially in the form of money, precious metals, jewels, etc.
• any person or thing considered very valuable

2. Confirm that treasures are indeed such things of value. However, let the students know that a treasure can also be something that has special meaning to someone. Share a personal treasure such as a special rock or a hand-crafted item you received as a gift. Tell the story behind the item and explain why you consider it a treasure. Ask if they can think of any treasures they have that aren't necessarily expensive.

It's fine for students to say that a pet or a person is a treasure.

3. Tell the students that treasures can also be small interesting objects that are found at home or outdoors. Let them know that they are going to begin to collect these kinds of treasures to use in the classroom. Ask if anyone has a collection at home. Get your students to start thinking about treasure items by showing a few things that you would like them to collect, such as buttons, shells, rocks, old keys, stamps, foreign coins, etc.

4. Hold up a treasure box to help students visually define the size of items that would fit into the boxes. Begin a class list of *small* items they could collect.

5. Show them one of the construction paper squares that they will use to help determine the size of objects that will fit into the box. Give each student one square to hold. Ask what things they can think of that are about that size. Add these new items to the class list.

6. Use a paper square to model how to measure a few objects (some larger, some smaller, and some the same size as the square) to see if they meet the criteria to fit in the box.

7. Tell the class that you would like them to bring in items from home to create treasure boxes at school. Explain clearly that the items they bring in will remain in the class and will not be returned. Also emphasize that there is NO need to BUY anything for these collections! Let them know that the treasures can be "recycled" from home. For example, items like canceled stamps, bottle caps, old buttons, rocks, shells, and bread tags do not cost anything to collect. Point out that by creating these collections, they are recycling and reusing things that might otherwise be thrown away.

One teacher had a collection of small boxes and gave each student one box to put their treasures in to bring to school. Another teacher gave each student a small recycled brown bag. A ziplock plastic bag also works well.

8. Answer any question about the collections. Tell students that they are going to take home a letter to share with their families to get their help in finding treasures at home. Give a letter to each student and have them attach the construction paper square to the letter.

9. Tell students to bring in items as soon as they can and that in one week they will begin to put their collected treasures into boxes. If you keep a class calendar with special events, you may want to mark the day that you want to begin putting the treasures in boxes.

10. Have a large box available to store the treasures your students bring in during the course of the week. You may also want to have small plastic bags so they can place their treasures in a bag and label them with their names.

Session 2: Filling the Boxes with Treasures

1. In an area away from the students' desks, have available the empty boxes and the marker for the treasure sorting, boxing, and box labeling. Also have some extra treasures available. Post the class list of treasures made in Session 1.

2. Have students gather their treasures from the large box and come to the designated area and sit in a circle. Distribute extra treasures to those students who need them.

3. Let students know this is the day to fill the boxes with treasures. Read the class list. Add any new items that they brought in that are not already on the list. Reread the list and as you do, ask for a show of hands to see if anyone brought in each item listed. If a few hands are raised for an item, label a box with the name of that item. If only one person has items for a box, wait until completing the list before you label a box for that item. At the end of the list, ask if there are any additional items that were brought in that were not on the list. Record these items.

Do not label boxes with the name of an item unless there are at least 10 items. Assure students that even though there may not be a box for every item they brought in at this time, more treasure boxes can be created later.

4. Place the labeled boxes in the center of the circle of students. Have students guess which boxes they think will have the most treasures.

5. Have one student choose a labeled box and walk that box around the perimeter of the circle to collect the appropriate treasures.

6. Continue with another student taking a second labeled box around to collect the next treasure item. You may want to have two boxes circulating at the same time to keep the process moving along.

7. After all the labeled boxes are filled, have students look at the remaining items that they're holding. Place those items in the center of the group. Can they be placed in a new box or an existing box or boxes? Decide as a class how to solve this problem in a way that allows the whole group to contribute to the decision.

8. Take a minute with the class to see how each treasure box was filled. Take this opportunity to do informal estimating. Ask, "Which box has the most?" "least?" Let students know that they can contribute to the boxes every day by bringing in additional items. Point out boxes that have only a few items.

9. Tell the class that even though individuals brought in specific treasures, the treasure collections now belong to the whole class. Let them know that in the days to follow they'll have many opportunities to explore and investigate the treasures.

10. After school, evaluate how many boxes are ready for use. To be of interest, a box for two students needs at least 25 items, and a box for four students needs at least 50 items. If your boxes fall short, here are some options:

- Use only the boxes that are ready and have only a part of your class begin with them the next day. You could have a sign up sheet ready so students know they will all have a chance to use them in the next few days.

- Be prepared to supplement your boxes with additional materials. For example, obtain different types of small pasta shapes and create duplicate treasure boxes of pasta.

- Continue to collect treasures as a class. Wait until enough is collected for each pair to have a box to share before beginning the activities.

Going Further

1. Journal Writing. Have the students close their eyes and think about a special treasure of their own. To help them, have them think about special places that they enjoyed visiting such as the beach or park or creek. Did they find a treasure there? Did someone give them a special item? Have them draw a picture of the treasure and then write or dictate why it is a treasure to them.

2. Share a Treasure. In addition to the small treasures that your students will be bringing in, you may want to give them an opportunity to bring in a special treasure to share that will NOT go into a box. These treasures might include quilts that have been passed down through the family, a photograph, a hand-crafted item, a well-loved stuffed animal, or a book. Brainstorm a list to help students see the diversity of items that could be considered special.

3. "Who Put the Treasure in the Treasure Box?" Change the words in the well-known chant, "Who Stole the Cookies from the Cookie Jar?" to "Who Put the Treasure in the Treasure Box?" Children love doing the chant and it's a handy transition activity throughout the unit.

4. Treasure Printing and Rubbings. Use treasures such as pasta shapes and natural objects to make prints with tempera paint. (Limiting the paints to two complementary

This is a great "get to know you" activity for the beginning of the school year.

A wonderful book that highlights a family treasure is The Keeping Quilt *by Patricia Polacco.*

colors produces a striking piece of artwork.) Sunprint
paper is another way to make terrific prints of collected
treasures. Use crayons to make rubbings of a variety of flat
treasures such as keys, coins, or buttons.

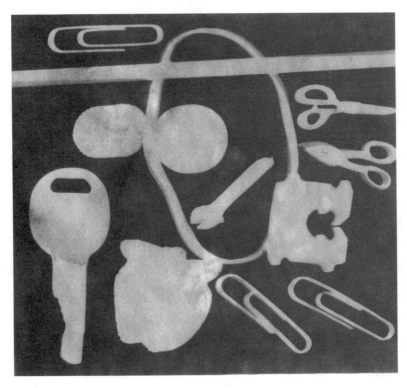

A sunprint of treasures.

Activity 2: Exploring Treasures

Overview

Once the treasure boxes are ready to use, the exploring begins! As with any new material, students need many opportunities to freely explore the treasure boxes. Your class will enjoy closely examining the treasures they've collected. In the process, they practice important math and science skills such as observing, comparing, organizing, and communicating. Exploring the treasures in an unstructured way will help prepare your students for more directed activities later on.

As the students explore the treasure boxes, they share new ideas about the treasures, discover similarities and differences, sort, count, measure, create patterns, articulate ideas, acquire new language, ask questions, develop cooperative work skills, and learn from their peers.

Free exploration also allows you to informally assess your students' skills and abilities. As an active observer, you will see firsthand their cooperative and independent work skills. You can also focus on specific skills and gain information about their prior knowledge.

The best thing about free exploration is that everyone is successful and works at their own ability level. Your students' curiosity is kindled and they have fun as they are given the opportunity to learn in their own unique way.

Provide at least a week for your students to explore the treasure boxes. They will, of course, continue to investigate the treasures as they move on to the more structured activities.

Beans   Louis
            Joeya

We have DiFFErent Kinds oF Beans.
Some Beans are Littel and Skinny.
Some Beans are DiFFErent Colors.
Some Beans are Big and Smal.
Some Beans are PurPL and Brown.
Some Beans are round and FLat.
Some Beans are BLak and wiet.
All Beans have BelyButtehs.
Some Beans are orange and wiet.
Some Beans are red and green.

What You Need

For the class:
- ❏ 8–16 filled treasure boxes
- ❏ (*optional*) 32 student journals **or** sheets of paper for recording observations

Getting Ready

1. Be sure that there are enough filled treasure boxes for each pair or group of four students to have their own box. Decide how you will organize students in pairs or groups.

2. As the students explore their treasures, you may want to observe for sorting and classifying skills, cooperative behavior, and problem solving skills.

3. Determine how the partners or groups will be given a treasure box to explore. Some possible methods include:

- You hand out the boxes to pairs of students. This method works especially well in kindergarten.

- Randomly select two or four names out of a hat to create pairs or groups of four. Then have the partners select a treasure box with which to work.

- Allow students to select their own partners or groups and choose a treasure box.

4. If your students will record their observations after their free exploration, decide what format to use. A few options include:

- With kindergarten and some first grade students, you may want to just have a group sharing where the students share their observations verbally and you record their ideas on the board or chart paper. Or you could use a tape recorder or students can dictate their ideas to you.

- Have the pair or group cooperatively record their discoveries on a sheet of paper. The record can include pictures.

- Have each student write or draw her discoveries in a journal.

- Enlist the help of students from upper grades (for example, some kindergartners have fifth grade "buddies") to record dictation from the kindergarten or first grade youngsters.

Exploring!

1. Tell the students that today they will be explorers. Ask them what an explorer does. Let them know they will explore a treasure box with a partner or in a group of four students.

2. Explain that their job is to find out all that they can about what is in their treasure box. Encourage them to use almost all of their senses—touch, sight, sound, and smell, but not taste—to help them investigate!

3. Since they will work with other students, ask what ground rules they'll need to establish for sharing the treasures. You may want to write a very simple list of basic rules that the class decides on.

4. Distribute the treasure boxes. Allow the students time to explore and investigate.

5. Circulate among the class and observe their explorations. Ask questions to promote more in-depth observations.

6. If the students need help focusing on the treasures, ask questions or pose challenges about the items. For example, "Find all the bottle caps with animals or stars on them" or "Find all the stamps with the number 29 or 32 on them."

If your students are experienced hand lens users, you may want to have hand lenses available. But for beginners, hand lenses are too distracting and need to be introduced separately.

Be sure to let students know that they will have many additional opportunities to work with the boxes and shouldn't feel badly if they don't get to work with their favorite box today.

You may observe some students using the treasures as a building material. This is fine. It is another way to discover the various attributes of the items.

Sharing and Recording Discoveries

1. After about 15–20 minutes, find out what the students have discovered. Have them share one or two things about the items in their boxes. Keep this discussion open-ended. If they have trouble coming up with discoveries, pose questions to help, such as:

- Did you find a favorite treasure? Describe it.

- What colors were your treasures?

- What shapes/sizes were your treasures?

- How did your treasures feel?

One teacher suggested that students take a mini-tour of all the boxes after about five minutes of exploration to see all the treasures. Another teacher had students rotate tables every five minutes.

2. Next, give the students an opportunity to walk around the room and take a peek at all the treasures being explored. Remind everyone to use their **eyes only.** Use your usual signal to get their attention and have the students return to their original treasure box.

3. If your students are going to record their discoveries, you may want to model how to record information about a treasure box using a box that everyone is familiar with. For example, tell them that you are going to record the discoveries about "Buttons" made by two partners, Chenoa and Jesse. Write the heading as follows:

Chenoa and Jesse   Date

Buttons
<u>   </u>

---

4. Ask the students what discoveries the partners could have made. They might say, "the buttons have holes" or "some are stars" or "some are shaped like fruit." Demonstrate how they might record their findings. For example:

Chenoa and Jesse   Date

Buttons

Buttons have 4 holes.

Some are shaped like stars.
(You can also model drawing the shapes.)

Some have two colors.

Some buttons are from sweaters.

---

5. Allow time for the students to record their discoveries.

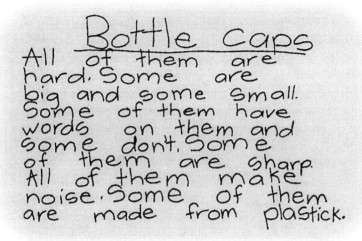

Bottle caps
All of them are hard. Some are big and some small. Some of them have words on them and some don't. Some of them are sharp. All of them make noise. Some of them are made from plastick.

by maria
Observations!

Rocks!
there smooth ones
Spongey ones and
art leand
Pink and Green
ones and
red
Shi ney ones

Beads
roend ones
Shiney ones
red ones
srcle ones
Smooth ones

6. After the discoveries are recorded, have the students return their treasures to the boxes and then join you in the group area.

7. Have the students read or tell what they wrote. You may want to record some of the discoveries they share. If a student giving a treasure report is having difficulty, assist her by asking questions, such as:

- What did you like best about the treasure?

- Did all the boxes have things of different colors? sizes? shapes?

- What did the treasures feel like?

8. After hearing each report on the treasure boxes, allow other students time to ask some questions.

9. Students never seem to tire of treasure exploring! Continue to have the boxes available for use during free choice times.

Every Key has a hole. Every Key has letters or Numbers on it. Most keys are silver or gold. Some keys are shaped wierd. Some Keys are small or big. All have lines down at the buttom. We found the tinyes key in the key box.

One teacher suggested that pairs or groups first record descriptive words to describe the treasures. Later, the whole class generated a list of adjectives from the work they did with their partners or groups.

Many teachers have had the treasure boxes available in a learning center to promote further exploration throughout the unit.

Going Further

1. More Collecting! Read *Aunt Ippy's Museum of Junk* by Rodney A. Greenblat to inspire more collecting of recycled items. In this story, a brother and sister visit their ecology-minded Aunt Ippy and her world-famous Museum of Junk which includes such treasures as a barrel of one-of-a-kind shoes and a sack of clocks. This story will raise awareness about recycling and reusing materials in new and different ways.

2. Treasure Activities and Games. Many teachers have suggested playing familiar games and doing activities with the treasures that focus on attributes to help "warm" students up for Activity 3. Here are three favorites:

   a. Guess My Pattern. In pairs, have one student generate a pattern using treasures from one box. Then have their partner decode and extend the pattern.

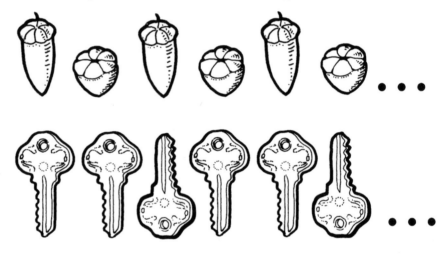

   b. Treasure Train. Have all students select one item from the treasure box in which they were working. Tell the students you want to make a "train" of treasures—a line of treasures with each treasure being a "car" of the train. Start by placing one treasure item in a central location to be the "engine." Brainstorm attributes of

Treasure Train

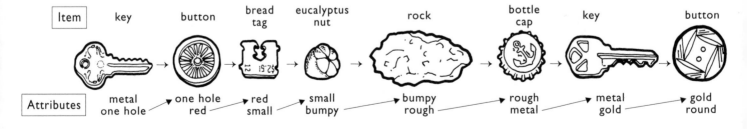

Item	key	button	bread tag	eucalyptus nut	rock	bottle cap	key	button
Attributes	metal one hole	one hole red	red small	small bumpy	bumpy rough	rough metal	metal gold	gold round

that treasure item. For example, if you put down a bottle cap, they might say it is red and black, has a star on it, has words written on it, etc. Ask if someone has a treasure that matches one of these attributes. Have that student place their treasure next to the first item and identify the matching attribute. Continue to have students take turns placing their treasure in the "train" and identifying the connecting attribute.

c. "Guess My Treasure" Game. Use an empty tissue box (cubical boxes work best for this) as a feely box. Place one treasure item in the box. Gather students in your group area. Have each student take a turn to reach inside the box—without peeking—and feel the object. As she feels the treasure inside the box, have her say one word to describe the treasure *without telling* what it is! You can record these words (which are the attributes of the treasure that can be felt) as the feely box is being circulated. After everyone has had a turn, review the attributes they gave and have the class guess what is inside the box. Finally, reveal the treasure! After playing once as a class, students can play the game with a partner or in small groups.

3. "I Spy" Books. The "I Spy" series of books by Jean Marzollo and Walter Wick contain photographs with incredible collections of objects—many that could come from a treasure box! Each two-page spread has rhyming verses to accompany it which ask the reader to find hidden objects in the photographs. This alone has children looking carefully at a set of objects and choosing specific ones. Young and older students alike hone their observation skills as they comb each page. In addition, each book has a theme that ties all the pages together and extra riddles related to the theme of each book. These riddles provide an extra challenge for students in grades 2 and 3. Many more questions or riddles could be posed to further delve into the attributes of the objects in the photographs. For example, you can ask questions that encourage students to search for objects of particular colors, shapes, sizes, types, uses, etc.

Activity 3: Treasures of Many Sorts

Overview

Even before you formally introduce sorting in this activity, many of your students may have already done some type of spontaneous sorting with the treasures as they explored the boxes. Now, the class as a whole focuses on the attributes of the treasures and finds ways to sort and classify them.

In Session 1, students begin with a whole class sorting activity. They sort an item common to all of them—their shoes. Shoes lend themselves to multiple sorts such as sorting by color, size, use of shoe (running, dress-up, play, etc.), and type of closure (lace, velcro, buckle, etc.). Using a personal item helps pique the students' interest in this initial sort.

Next, in Session 2, students work with a partner to sort and classify treasures from one box. After all students complete at least one sort, they share their methods of sorting. This can provide additional sorting ideas. When students sort the same treasure in more than one way, they use higher level and divergent thinking skills along with logic, language, and organizational skills.

In Session 3, second and third grade students are given the challenge of sorting treasures using Venn diagrams. This requires students to focus on more than one attribute at a time as they organize treasures into groups. They first participate in creating a Venn diagram guided by the teacher. This models when a Venn diagram is needed and how to create one. Next, pairs of students create their own Venn diagrams. This is a good way to both introduce and reinforce student experience with Venn diagrams as a tool to organize and interpret data.

As your students go through the sessions in this activity, they have opportunities for mathematical experiences in the following areas: number (used in context and for meaningful computation), geometry (as they explore the attributes), logic and language (as they sort and classify), statistics (as they observe and interpret the data organized), and discrete mathematics (as they organize a finite number of objects into Venn diagrams). The "Going Further" section includes other sorting and classifying activities in varying degrees of difficulty. These can help you challenge your students to "go further."

Some students may have sorted shoes before, but teachers who tested these activities assured us that their students were excited and enthusiastic about sorting and resorting their shoes.

Divergent thinking involves looking at the many different ways to approach and solve a problem. Sometimes, it means not following the apparent solution path! This allows students to be open to new processes in solving problems.

A Venn diagram is a way to organize a set (group) of objects. It consists of two or more overlapping circles. See page 29 for a Venn diagram made using a set of buttons.

What You Need

For the class:

For Session 1:
- ❏ 1 shoe from each student
- ❏ chart paper
- ❏ 1 marker

For Session 2:
- ❏ 16 filled treasure boxes
- ❏ 1 sheet of 12" x 18" construction paper
- ❏ several sheets of chart paper for recording attributes
- ❏ 1 marker
- ❏ 32 student journals **or** sheets of paper
- ❏ 32 pencils
- ❏ (*optional*) trays, small containers, cups, or egg cartons for sorting treasures that may roll

For Session 3:
- ❏ 1 treasure box (see #6 in "Getting Ready")
- ❏ 16 filled treasure boxes
- ❏ 1 sheet of 12" x 18" construction paper
- ❏ 3 pieces of 2" x 4" paper to label the Venn diagram
- ❏ chart paper
- ❏ 1 marker
- ❏ 16 cups or other containers to hold a subset of treasure
- ❏ 16 36" lengths of yarn in one color* for Venn diagrams
- ❏ 16 36" lengths of yarn in another color* for Venn diagrams
- ❏ 16 small plastic bags (for yarn loops)
- ❏ 32 student journals **or** sheets of paper
- ❏ 32 pencils

*Be sure the two colors of yarn are very distinct.

Getting Ready

1. Depending upon your students' attention spans and the time available in your schedule, decide if you will do **Sessions 1 and 2** on the same day.

2. For **Sessions 2 and 3,** consider how you will pair students and how you will assign the treasure boxes.

3. Before you begin **Session 2,** gather one treasure box (one that is filled with objects of varied and distinct colors—plastic animals or other types of plastic objects work well); the construction paper; several sheets of chart paper; a marker; and either student journals or paper for students to record sorts.

4. If you've decided to use them for **Session 2,** gather cups, trays, egg cartons, or other similar containers for the students to put their sorted treasures in.

5. **For Session 3,** make yarn loops for the Venn diagrams. Tie the ends of each individual yarn length together to form a loop. Place one yarn loop of each color into a small plastic bag.

6. Decide what treasure item you will use for the demonstration to introduce Venn diagrams to the whole class. This is the same item that *all* of your students will use to create their first Venn diagrams. You will need about 25 items per pair of students. Since it is not likely that there will be enough in any one treasure box, have students help to collect more of one specific item, such as stamps, bottle caps, pasta, buttons, etc. For example, if you have 32 students, you will need 16 cups with 25 pieces of treasure in each for a total of 400 pieces of treasure.

7. Before **Session 3,** gather the treasure box you will use, the construction paper, and two yarn loops. Put about 25 pieces of treasure in 16 cups so that each pair of students will have the same treasure to work with as you did. Have journals (or paper) available for students to record their Venn diagrams.

8. Have the other treasure boxes available for creating Venn diagrams.

Session 1: Shoe Sort

1. Gather the students in a group area away from their desks or tables. Tell them they are going to sort their shoes.

2. Have everyone remove one shoe and examine it. Ask them to share and compare their observations with a neighbor. Next, have everyone place a shoe right in front of themselves so that it is visible to the rest of the group.

3. Ask students to describe their shoes. You are likely to hear descriptions that include: colors, type of closure (laces, slip-on, velcro), shoe material (leather, cloth, plastic), use for the shoe (running shoe, dress-up), shoe style (high-top or low), or patterns on the soles of their shoes. Record their responses on the chart paper and tell them that what they described are the characteristics or *attributes* of the shoes.

4. Tell students that you want to sort the shoes into groups using **one** attribute. Allow them to choose (or you can decide) the attribute. For example, using the type of closure as the attribute for the sort, ask for one shoe with each type of closure to "label" the groups, such as laces, buckles, slip on, and velcro.

5. Once the groups are labeled, encourage students to predict which group will have the most and the fewest shoes. Sort the shoes, one by one, by going around the circle. Let each student place his or her shoe in the appropriate group.

6. After about half the shoes have been placed into a group, have the students make observations about the groups of shoes. Give them an opportunity to rethink their initial predictions about which group will have the most and fewest.

7. Continue placing shoes until everyone has put a shoe into a group. Ask questions about the numbers of shoes in each group, such as "Which group has the most shoes?" "fewest?" "Do any groups have the same number of shoes?" Be sure to count the number of shoes in each group to check their responses.

8. Refer back to the list of attributes. Ask if there are other ways to sort the shoes. Record any new ideas. Tell students that they will do another shoe activity in a few days. For now, have the students take back their own shoes in an orderly manner.

A good book is often a wonderful way to launch an activity. There are many books that illustrate the diversity of shoes and/or their uses. Using photographs by Rosemarie Hausherr, Ron Roy's book, Whose Shoes Are These? *features culturally diverse children wearing adult shoes that serve different purposes.* Shoes, Shoes, Shoes, *by Ann Morris with photographs by Ken Heyman, looks at shoes worn worldwide. There is a wealth of storybooks that feature shoes that would also serve as an entryway to shoe sorting. See the "Literature Connections" section for several listings.*

Session 2: Sorting Treasures

Sorting Treasures with the Whole Class

1. Gather the students in a group area away from their desks. Pour the contents of a treasure box onto a sheet of construction paper so that it will be easily visible to all students. Ask for some of the attributes of the treasure. Students are likely to suggest such attributes as color, size shape, kind, and texture.

2. Tell them you are going to sort the treasure. You may want to choose **color** as the attribute that you use to demonstrate, as color is easily visible. Ask the students to describe the colors of the treasure items.

3. As they mention a color, select one item of that color from the treasures on the construction paper. Place it by itself away from the other treasures. Repeat this for all the colors. You now have one treasure that "labels" each color group. Sort the rest of the treasure by color.

4. Ask questions about the sorted treasures, such as "Which group has the largest number of items?" "The fewest number?" Estimate and count the number in each color group. Use this opportunity to practice counting by twos or fives.

5. Have a student review how the treasure was sorted. Then push the treasures together to create one large group of treasures. Ask how the treasure could be sorted in another way. On chart paper record the list of attributes they suggest for sorting.

Sorting Treasures with a Partner

1. Tell your students that now they will have an opportunity to sort the treasures in one box with a partner. Review the class list of attributes used to sort. Tell the students they could also come up with a new way to sort if they want.

2. Let them know that after they have sorted their treasure, both partners should raise their hands. You will then come to them and take a peek at their sorts.

3. Ask the students to sit with their partner. Distribute a treasure box to each pair. Allow them time to discuss the attributes of their treasures and to sort the items.

There are many books that can be used as a springboard into sorting activities. See the "Literature Connections" section.

Many other GEMS guides include sorting and classification. In Liquid Explorations, students sort and classify a collection of liquids while in Tree Homes, students sort toy bears by various attributes. In Sifting Through Science, students sort and graph items by whether they float or sink and whether or not they're magnetic.

To keep your students focused, be sure to do this sort at a brisk pace. You may want to make a purposeful mistake so your students can correct the placement of a treasure.

4. Circulate around the room to observe and ask questions. After most students have finished, use your usual signal to get the attention of the class.

5. Ask, "How did you sort your treasures?" Encourage them to fully explain their sorts. After each description, ask if other pairs sorted in a similar way. As they share, record any new ways to sort on the class list.

6. After this discussion, have students focus back on their treasures and continue by *sorting their treasures a new way.*

7. Have students write down and/or illustrate one way they sorted their treasures—either in a journal or on a sheet of paper.

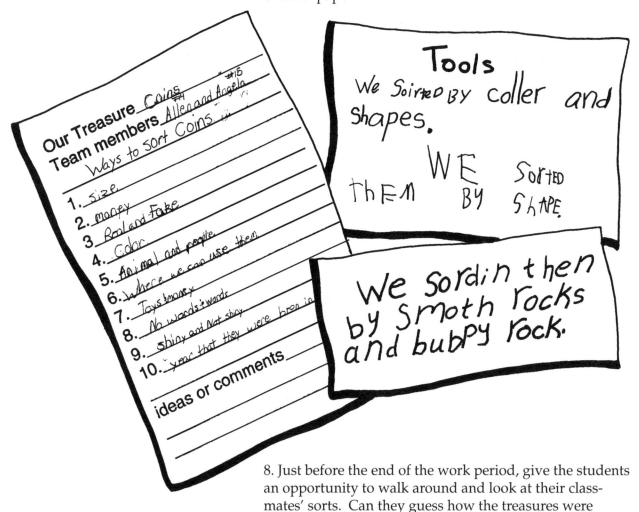

Our Treasure Coins #15
Team members Allen and Angela
Ways to Sort Coins

1. size.
2. money
3. Real and Fake
4. Color.
5. Animal and people.
6. where we can use them.
7. Toys money
8. No woods + words
9. shiny and Not shiny
10. year that they were born in

ideas or comments

Tools
We Sorted By coller and shapes.
WE Sorted
ThEM BY ShAPE.

We sordin then by Smoth rocks and bubby rock.

8. Just before the end of the work period, give the students an opportunity to walk around and look at their classmates' sorts. Can they guess how the treasures were sorted? When they are through, ask the students to put their treasures back in the boxes.

9. Refer back to the list of attributes used to sort. Ask if there are any other attributes that they used to sort that are not on the list. Add to the list as needed.

To organize the observation of classmates' work, one teacher used the idea of a "tour." She was the tour guide and the children followed behind her.

10. Continue to have the boxes available for students to use when they choose.

Session 3: Venn Diagrams to Sort Treasure—A Challenge for Grades 2–3

Introducing Venn Diagrams

1. Gather the students in the group area. Tell them that they are going to sort treasures a new way. Pour the contents of a treasure box, such as buttons, onto the sheet of construction paper. Ask the students to describe the buttons. Remind them that these descriptions are the **attributes** of the buttons.

2. Tell them that together you are going to sort the buttons into two smaller groups in a new way using yarn loops. Set out the two yarn loops into distinct circles. Using the 2" x 4" paper, label one circle "Round" and the other circle "Small."

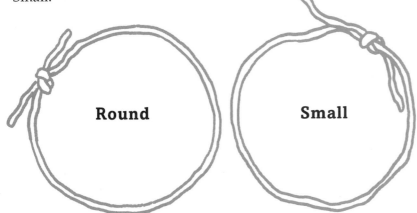

3. Hold up a large, round button. Ask where it belongs. Put it in the circle labeled "Round."

4. Choose a small, non-round button next. Ask where it belongs. Put it in the appropriate circle.

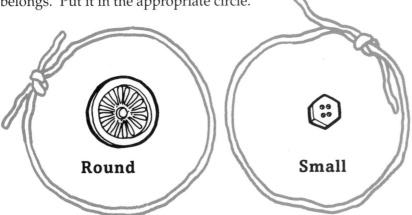

In the GEMS guide, Investigating Artifacts, Venn diagrams are introduced to sort found objects.

If your students are ready to use the vocabulary of "set theory" (of which Venn diagrams are a part), you may want to introduce the word "set" to describe the group of buttons to be sorted. It refers to the entire group of buttons.

You may want to consider some other ways to introduce the basic idea of Venn diagrams. In a physically active fashion, you could have the class play a game outside. On the playground, draw a large rectangle with chalk, and then use a large rope to form a circle inside the rectangle. Have a group of students be inside the rectangle and then give instructions, such as: "Run into the circle if you like_____" or "Run into the circle if have have_____." This should help provide a basic intuitive sense of Venn diagrams. In class, you could do a similar introduction. Draw the loop within the rectangle on the board then give the class some examples and ask them to provide others, such as having all items with the color red inside the circle, and all that are not red outside of it, and so on.

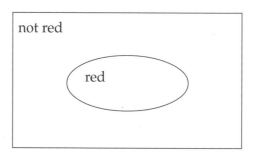

5. Continue with a few more buttons that ONLY fit into one of the two designated circles.

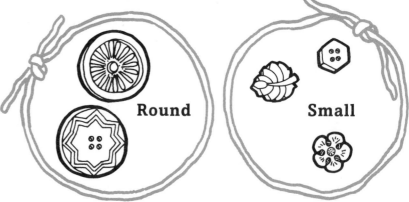

6. Then hold up a button that is BOTH round and small. Ask which group it belongs in. Some students may say round. Others may say small. Still others will see the dilemma and say that it belongs in both groups! Pull the yarn loops together to create an overlapping area and label it "Round and Small." (In set theory, this overlapping area is known as the "intersection" of these two sets.) Place the round and small button in the overlapping area.

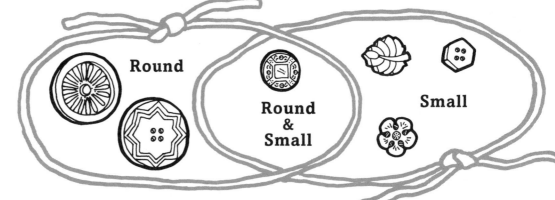

7. Continue with a few more buttons that belong in one of these three groups. When you get to a button that does not fit into any group, such as a large, square button (or any button that is large and not round), ask the students where it could be placed. [It is placed outside of the yarn loops.]

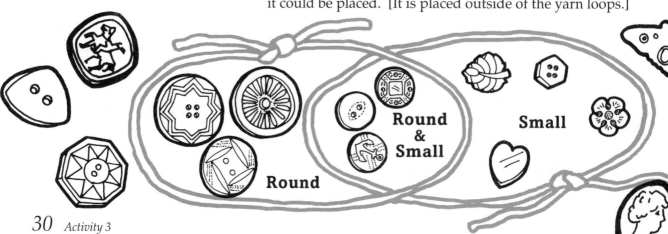

8. Continue until there are at least 20 buttons sorted into their appropriate places in the Venn diagram. Tell the students that you used a **Venn diagram** to organize the buttons. Ask if anyone has ever heard of a Venn diagram. Tell them that a Venn diagram is a tool used to organize information. It uses circles or loops to organize or sort things. Venn diagrams can be used for many more things than buttons.

9. Ask for a volunteer to describe what this Venn diagram tells us. You are likely to hear statements such as "Some buttons are round and some are small and some are both round and small." You may also hear comments such as "There are more round buttons than small buttons." Be sure that statements like this last one are accurate! In counting the buttons in this type of sort, you need to count the round buttons both in the part of the yarn loop that has only round buttons as well as those in the intersection! Be sure to encourage students to explain their thinking.

Making an Intersecting Venn Diagram with a Partner

1. Tell students that, working with a partner, they will now sort a group of buttons using a Venn diagram. Ask what other ways, besides "round" and "small," there might be to create a Venn diagram using buttons.

2. On chart paper, list their ideas for two *distinct* groups that also overlap, for example: "a color and a shape," "a color and a size," "a color and a texture," etc.

3. You may want to ask what groups would *not* work with a Venn diagram. [Any two distinct groups that do not overlap wouldn't work, such as round and square buttons, two-holed and four-holed buttons, and in some cases, two distinct colors of buttons (assuming no buttons have both colors).]

4. Send the students to their work areas and distribute buttons and yarn loops. Circulate and observe students. Ask them to explain their Venn diagrams to you.

5. After all the students have made Venn diagrams on their desks, ask them to walk around and observe the Venn diagrams other students have made.

6. Gain the attention of the class and ask them to return to their seats. Ask if the Venn diagrams helped them to determine how the treasures were sorted. Have them explain how the diagram helped or made it harder.

Don't worry if your students do not immediately grasp the idea of Venn diagrams. In some cases, the students will need more practice, while in other cases, they may not be developmentally ready for the conceptual framework of Venn diagrams. Even adults sometimes have difficulty!

In common usage, the term "Venn diagram" is often used to refer to two circles containing objects or data that intersect and overlap when differing objects share a common attribute (as shown in the illustrations). Technically speaking, however, even one circle with objects or data in it can be considered a Venn diagram, as can two circles with objects or data in them which do not intersect. In these treasure box activities there is a strong emphasis on encouraging students to use logical thinking skills to select attributes which do result in an intersection. Such an intersection is of course one of the most useful and revealing aspects of Venn diagrams.

Some students may try to create groups by size. In this case, there is no overlapping area. Students may also try color. Again, there may not be an overlapping area unless the objects in the treasure box are multicolored. Use this as an opportunity for learning and focusing on attributes. Students have to hold more than one attribute in mind as they sort in this way. In general, choosing two quite distinct attributes possessed by a number of the items is more likely to lead to an intersection. If this type of sorting seems too challenging for your students, save it for a time after they have had more practice sorting in simpler ways.

7. Provide time for the students to record their Venn diagrams in their journals or on sheets of paper.

Venn Diagram Challenge!

1. Tell students that their next challenge will be to create an intersecting Venn diagram with a partner using one of the other treasure boxes (other than the buttons or whatever item the whole class used).

2. Review the class list of the ways to create Venn diagrams from their experience with buttons. Ask for any additional methods to create Venn diagrams.

3. Distribute a treasure box to each pair of students to create Venn diagrams.

4. As students are working, circulate and ask questions about their work.

5. When all partners have completed a Venn diagram, have students take a "tour" of the work their classmates did. Challenge them to determine how the treasures were sorted in each Venn diagram.

6. Refocus as a class and ask for observations about the Venn diagrams. Ask if there were additional ways to create Venn diagrams to add to the class list.

7. Provide time for the students to record their Venn diagrams in their journals or on sheets of paper.

As you "tour," you may discover that some students did not accurately make intersecting Venn diagrams. Use this as a teaching and learning opportunity. Have the students who created the Venn explain their thinking. Then ask the class if they agree with that thinking. If no one is able to explain the problem with the Venn diagram, contribute to the discussion in a positive way and explain it yourself. Frame this as a way of learning about Venn diagrams. Remember, learning from our mistakes is a powerful tool and a useful lesson in itself!

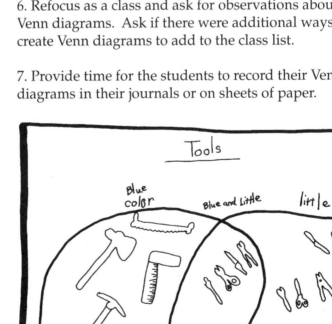

Jamie and Ivan

shells

Bumpy

Bumpy
← and →
White

White

Keys

Brown
With Triangle

Browns

With Triangles

Analyzing Venn Diagram Data (for older students)

1. After several experiences with Venn diagrams, third grade students can be challenged with questions that relate to the information that the Venn diagram provides. For example, consider the following Venn diagram of buttons.

2. Pose questions such as:

- How many buttons are in the group of **large** buttons that are **not black?**

- If you counted all the **large** buttons, how many would you have?

- How many buttons are in the group of **black** buttons that are **not large?**

- If you counted all the **black** buttons, how many would you have?

- How many buttons are in the group of buttons that are **both** large and black?

- How many buttons in this collection of buttons are **neither** black nor large?

- If you counted **all** buttons, how many would you have?

As students count the buttons in this way, they are doing discrete mathematics. Discrete mathematics has to do with counting principles and emphasizes a countable number—often arranged in sets, arrays, and other types of diagrams. Each group on this Venn diagram is distinct and countable—there is a finite number. In addition, by using the Venn diagram as an organizational tool, each button has one unique placement on the diagram, though it may need to be counted more than one time when analyzing the data. So when your students are doing this activity, not only are they working on logic and language as well as number, they are also doing discrete mathematics.

Going Further

1. Computer Connection. After doing concrete sorting with the treasure boxes, students can use the Kid Pix® drawing program to sort using the "rubber stamp" feature. The stamp collection includes a variety of objects such as animals, foods, vehicles, tools, etc. When the students begin, have them draw a circle on their monitor. Inside the circle they can "stamp" a selection of related objects such as fruits and "stamp" non-fruit items outside of the circle. Next, they can create two (or more) distinct groups such as plants and animals. After second and third graders have had experience making intersecting Venn diagrams with real objects, you may want them to create intersecting Venn diagrams with the Kid Pix stamps. First, have them draw two intersecting circles. Next they need to decide on the two groups. For example, they can stamp all of the red objects in one circle and all of the fruit in another. In the intersection there will be the red fruit!

2. Additional Ways to Sort

   a. Find a Match. With kindergartners, even before sorting items into many groups, young children can find matches or pairs in the treasure boxes. This helps them to focus on attributes and details of the treasure— a first step in sorting.

   b. Successive Sorting. Take a box of treasure. Sort it into *just two* distinct groups such as red treasures and not red treasures. Then sort those two groups again by another attribute such as bumpy and smooth. Now there will be four groups—red and bumpy, red and smooth, not red and bumpy, and not red and smooth. Try to use another attribute to further sort each group. If you can, there will be eight groups. If a group cannot be formed, students will be introduced to the empty set.

3. Sorting at Home. To bridge the learning from school to home, have students sort "collections" that are commonly found in their homes. One teacher had his students sort kitchen utensils—both those for eating and those for cooking. Other collections to sort include: socks, shoes, writing tools, books, buttons, coins, beans, etc.

Kid Pix® is available for use with IBM/Tandy, Windows, and Macintosh systems. For more information on this computer program, contact Brøderbund Software, 500 Redwood Blvd., Novato, CA 94948-6121, (415) 382-4700.

The GEMS Teacher's Guide Frog Math: Predict, Ponder, Play *diagrams how to create successive sorts using buttons.*

Activity 4: Treasure Graphs

Overview

In our daily lives we encounter data in many forms—from the nutritional statistics on cereal boxes to a variety of graphs in newspapers. In this activity, students use the treasure boxes to examine data and organize the treasure items using graphs. By introducing data analysis through these fun and familiar treasure boxes, this important area of mathematics becomes accessible and relevant.

In Session 1, students begin with a whole group graphing activity using their shoes. After choosing an attribute, such as the type of closure, students create a large graph. Next, they make observations about the data on their shoe graph.

In Session 2, pairs of students sort and organize the treasures using graphing grids. The graphing grids are purposefully open-ended in design so that the students have an opportunity to strategize how to best represent the data. They also interpret the data from the treasure graphs by making observations and "true statements" about how the treasure is organized. Next, students create a new graph with the same treasure using a different attribute to organize it. By graphing the same treasures twice, students see that the same data can be organized in more than one way. The two concrete graphs look different and provide different information.

While doing these graphing activities your students are developing their logical thinking as well as divergent thinking skills as they work with data. The activity provides students with concrete experience using the important mathematical strand of statistics. In addition, students practice and reinforce their number skills including one-to-one correspondence, counting, addition, subtraction, and comparing numbers.

In the GEMS Teacher's Guide, Sifting Through Science, *students use graphs to organize the results of science explorations. In addition, the guide contains a special background section on graphing.*

What You Need

For the class:
- ❏ 16 filled treasure boxes
- ❏ 1 shoe from each student
- ❏ 30 bread tags or another easily visible treasure
- ❏ 1 sheet of 12" x 18" construction paper
- ❏ a 48" x 108" piece of butcher paper for a large class graphing grid
- ❏ 1 ruler/yardstick
- ❏ 1 permanent dark marker
- ❏ 34 small graphing grids (master on page 91)
- ❏ 32 student journals **or** sheets of paper for recording graphs

Getting Ready

1. Plan which treasure boxes will be distributed to which pairs of students for the graphing in Session 2.

2. Make the large class graphing grid as follows:

   a. Cut a piece of butcher paper to 48" wide x 108" long. The following steps involve a series of folds to make a grid created by the fold lines.

48"

108"

   b. Fold the paper in half to measure 48" x 54". Crease the fold. Again, fold the paper in half to measure 48" x 27". Crease this fold.

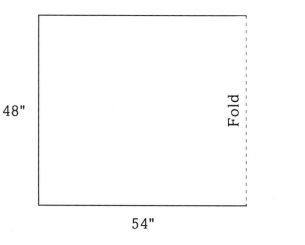

48"

Fold

54"

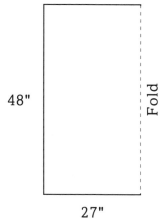

48"

Fold

27"

c. Continue folding in the same manner—this time fold the 27" length into thirds. The paper will measure 48" x 9". Crease the folds.

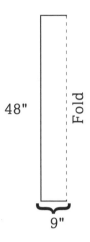

48" Fold

9"

d. Open up the paper to its full size. There will be 11 fold lines across the width of the paper.

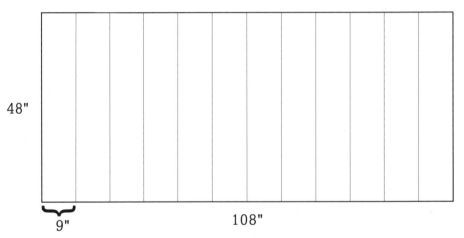

48"

9" 108"

e. Now fold the paper in half to measure 24" x 108". Crease the fold. Fold this 24" width into thirds. It will measure 8" x 108". Crease the folds.

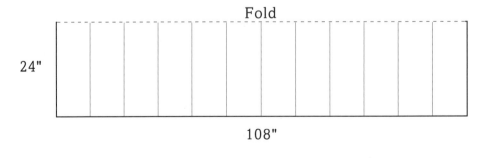

Fold

24"

108"

Fold

8"

108"

f. Open up the paper to its full size. There will be a grid created by the fold lines. There will be 11 fold lines that go across the width of the paper and five fold lines that go across the length of the paper.

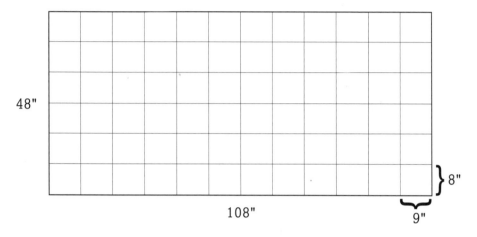

48"

108"

} 8"

9"

g. With a permanent dark marker and ruler/yardstick, draw lines on top of all the fold lines to create a grid with 8" x 9" rectangles. It will measure 6 rectangles wide by 12 rectangles long.

3. When you teach Session 1, have the large graphing grid available.

4. Duplicate 32 small graphing grids from the master on page 91. For Session 2, each pair of students needs one grid to begin graphing treasures and then may need an additional grid as their graph expands. Duplicate two extra small graphing grids for your class demonstration. The graphing grid is open-ended on two sides so additional copies can be attached to enlarge the grid.

5. When you teach Session 2, have available a treasure box, the construction paper, and two small graphing grids. Have 16 small graphing grids ready for the pairs of students and the 16 additional grids that the students may need in an accessible spot.

This large class graph has been used successfully to graph most children's shoes in grades K–3. Larger shoes can be placed on the diagonal in each box.

Session 1: Graphing Shoes

1. Gather the students in a group area away from their desks or tables. Tell them they are going to use their shoes again for an activity. Have everyone remove one shoe and place it right in front of themself so it is visible to the rest of the group.

In the previous activity, students organized treasures by sorting them into groups. In this activity, students take the next step and use an attribute to organize, first shoes and then treasures, on graphs. For kindergartners and those students with less experience, it may be better for you to actually sort the shoes first, and then use the graphing grid as a tool to further organize the sort.

2. Drawing upon their knowledge from the previous sorting activities, ask the students to recall how they sorted their shoes. Then ask for additional ways to describe the characteristics or attributes of the shoes.

3. Lay the large graphing grid on the floor in the middle of the group. Tell the students that they are going to use this tool—a graphing grid—to help organize their shoes into groups by a particular attribute. Decide on the attribute they will use to graph the shoes, such as type of closure.

4. "Label" each row with a type of shoe closure. Place one shoe with laces in a square at the end of one row. Then, in a row adjacent to the shoe with laces, place a shoe with velcro. Place a slip-on shoe in an empty square, adjacent to the velcro shoe. Add shoes with any other type of closure, such as buckles, to the remaining rows.

5. Have students predict which attribute (type of closure) will have the most/fewest shoes. Then go around the circle of students and have each student, one by one, place their shoes in the appropriate row. Stop along the way to ask a few comparing questions about the graph. Encourage students to observe how the graph changes as more shoes are added. Give students a chance to adjust their predictions as they get more information.

6. When all the shoes are on the graph, ask for observations about the graph. Then pose questions, such as the following, so students will continue to count and compare the number of shoes in the different categories.

- Which row has the most shoes? the fewest?

- Are there any rows that have the same number of shoes?

- How many more shoes with laces are there than slip-on shoes?

- How many shoes have velcro?

- How many fewer shoes are slip-on than velcro?

- If you add the tie shoes and the velcro shoes, how many will you have?

- How many total shoes are on the graph?

- What information does this graph give us?

7. Tell students that when they're answering these questions, they are making "true statements" about the data on the graph. True statements are factual statements about the data on the graph. These include number and comparison statements.

8. For older students or those who have had a lot of experience graphing, you may want to pose some questions that go further than the actual data on the graph, such as:

- What is the most popular type of shoe closure?

- Why are there so few slip-on shoes on the graph?

- Since most people wore tie shoes, are tie shoes the best shoes? Why or why not?

- If we did this graph tomorrow, would we get the same results? Why or why not?

- Who would be interested in the results of this graph?

Note: These questions involve interpretations of the data. These questions challenge students to think and most importantly to see the difference between factual information gained from the graph and interpretation of that information.

9. Have the students collect their shoes in an orderly manner.

Looking at a graph of bottle caps organized by the pictures on them, some true statements could include the following: "There are seven bottle caps with stars on them." "There are more bottle caps with animals than there are with stars." "There are five fewer bottle caps with crowns on them than with animals."

*Statements that would **not** be true would include: "Bottle caps with animals on them are better than any others." "No one really likes drinks that come in bottles with crowns on the caps." "The bottle caps with the stars are the prettiest." These statements reflect opinions or personal preferences about the bottle caps.*

Do not be alarmed if your students do not "get" the difference between true statements and interpretations at first. The more experience they have with graphs, the more the difference will become clear to them.

Session 2: Graphing Treasures

Demonstrate How to Graph Treasures

If you choose to do Session 2 right after the shoe graph, you may also want to do a quick movement activity or game before continuing.

1. Gather the students in a circle again. Pour out about 30 bread tags (or another treasure that is easily visible to all in the circle area) onto the sheet of construction paper.

2. Tell the students that you are going to organize the bread tags in a way similar to what they did with their shoes. This time instead of using a large class graphing grid, you are going to use a smaller graphing grid to organize the bread tag treasure.

3. Hold up a small graphing grid. Ask how it is similar to the large graphing grid and how it is different. Tell them you are going to use it to graph the bread tags by color. (Either color or size work well to demonstrate this activity to the whole class.)

4. Place the small grid in the center of the group. "Label" each row by putting a bread tag of a different color in the first square at the end of each row.

(red)
(green)
(blue)
(white)
(yellow)
(orange)

5. Next, place the bread tags, one by one according to color, on the grid with the assistance of student volunteers.

6. As you go along you may want to ask students to predict which color bread tag will have the most and fewest. It may change as you go along.

You may also want to make a deliberate mistake with the placement of a bread tag to give the students an opportunity to correct your error. This technique will help students stay "tuned in" as you graph.

7. When you have placed all the bread tags on the grid, ask for observations and true statements about it.

8. Ask students for other ways to graph the bread tags. If your class needs another example to get them started, choose another very visible way to graph the bread tags, such as by size. Graph them again on the second small graphing grid. Ask questions about this graph.

Students Graph Treasures

1. Tell your students that with a partner they are going to graph treasures in a similar way. Each pair will receive a box of treasure and a small grid. Their task is to take a handful—or at least 30 pieces—of treasure and talk about the attributes. Then using an agreed upon attribute, graph the treasure on the grid.

2. When they are done, they should raise their hands so you can take a look at their graphs. While waiting, they can discuss the graph and make observations and true statements about it.

3. Pass out the treasure boxes and small graphing grids to each pair of students and ask them to begin. Circulate while your students are busy graphing. Help students orient their grids and respond to any problems that arise. Pose questions about their graphs when they have completed them.

4. After they have graphed their treasure one way, encourage students to reorganize the treasure and graph it again using a new attribute.

Depending upon what attribute your students use to graph, some may need a second graphing grid to enlarge their graphs. Additionally, you may notice some students orienting their grids in a different way than you did with bread tags. That's okay. Just be sure that they label and fill the grid appropriately.

5. When everyone has created a graph or two, give the students an opportunity to walk around the room and look at all the different graphs.

6. Depending upon your students experience and abilities with graphing, choose the appropriate method of permanently recording the data from the treasure graphs they created.

*A **concrete or real-object graph** is created by organizing real objects on a graphing grid. The first type of representational graph that students create from a concrete graph is a **pictorial graph**. In a pictorial graph, students use another identical graphing grid sheet and draw pictures in the boxes to represent the objects on the graph. Next, older students can create a **symbolic graph** in which the graph is recorded in an abstract way—such as using "x"s to represent the objects on the graph.*

a. Pictorial Graph (recommended for Grades 1–2): Either individually or with their partners, have students draw a picture of their graphs. Then they can write at least three true statements about their graphs and one question that can be answered by looking at the graph.

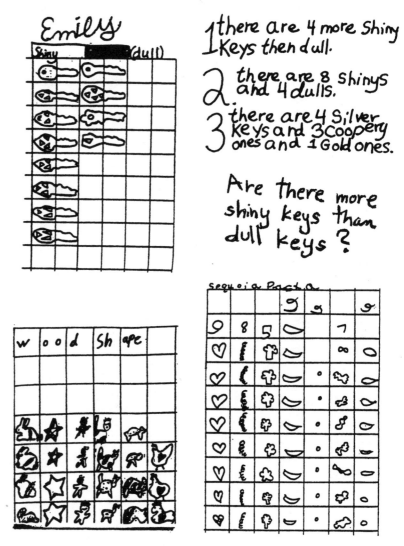

b. Symbolic Graph (recommended for Grades 2–3): Students can record the data by labeling the graph and then placing "x"s (or check marks or dots) to represent the data that is on the treasure graph they created. Then they can write at least three true statements about their graphs and two questions that can be answered by the data on the recorded graph.

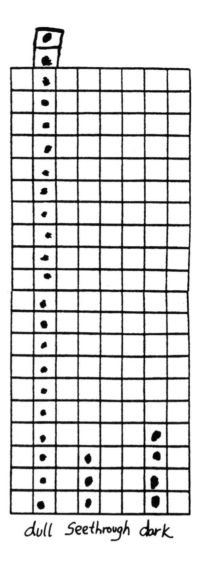

dull Seethrough dark

ROCKS
1. there are 22 dull rocks.
2. there are 18 more dull then dark
3. there are 3 see throu

Darren

How many dull rocks are in this collection?
How many more dark rocks are there than see-through rocks?

Going Further

1. Graphing Hats from Home and Create a Cap. A personal hat can serve as another high interest item—similar to shoes—to use for sorting and graphing with the entire class. Have students bring hats to school. Brainstorm ways to describe the hats and their attributes. Then graph the hats in different ways. Alternately, students can "create a cap" at school out of a variety of materials. These hats can be sorted and graphed as well as worn in a parade! There are many children's books to launch this activity including *Hats, Hats, Hats* by Ann Morris and the traditional *Caps for Sale* by Esphyr Slobodkina. For information on these and other "graphing" books, please see the "Literature Connections" section.

2. Graphing Items of Personal Interest. Choose other personal, high-interest items that students have at home or school to graph in more than one way, such as by color, size, shape, use, or texture. For example:

a. From home, each student can bring one item. Decide on a type of item you want each student to bring—such as a toy animal, a vehicle, or an item made out of wood. Brainstorm ways to graph these treasures from home, and then graph them in a variety of ways.

b. In the classroom, students can choose from common shared materials such as writing tools, math manipulatives, or their art pieces. Choose one type of item to graph. Have each student find one of these items. Brainstorm ways to graph these items and create graphs in more than one way.

3. Survey Graphs (for Grades 2–3). The book *The Best Vacation Ever* by Stuart J. Murphy introduces survey graphs in a meaningful context. In the book, a young girl decides that her busy family needs a vacation. To help determine what vacation would meet all their needs, she surveys her family and then analyzes her data only to discover that the best vacation ever is in their own backyard! The young girl's problem-solving and data-collecting skills can be translated to the classroom setting. Students can generate survey questions and poll themselves and then analyze the data they collect. Families can be involved in these survey questions linking home and school. When a class needs to make a difficult choice, surveys can be used to help make a decision.

In the GEMS guides Liquid Explorations *and* Secret Formulas, *there are suggestions for survey graphs on the favorite types of beverages among students.*

Activity 5: Treasure Maps

Overview

In this activity, students play a hidden treasure game that gives them experience with coordinates. In Session 1, they use cards with coordinates to determine the location of treasure on a map. This is an inviting way to familiarize the students with the grid—everyone is successful! It also prepares them for the game in Session 2. After all the treasure is found, they may sort and classify their treasures or simply enjoy looking them over and then playing again.

In Session 2, there is a new twist on the hunt for first through third graders—finding the hidden treasure becomes a challenging game! Using a file folder as a screen, one person "hides" treasure on the map. Their partner has to find the treasure by asking about specific coordinates. The "guessing" partner uses a map to record her guesses until she finds all the treasure. Next, the two players switch roles, and play again. As students play this game several times, they may want to try to find the treasure in as few moves as possible. You are likely to notice strategies evolving as students try to do this.

The game format interweaves strong mathematical learning. In these games, students familiarize themselves with a coordinate grid—a mathematical tool that is vital to the graphing they will encounter later. They also develop mapping skills and practice cooperative work skills. In Session 2, students use logical and divergent thinking skills as they develop and test strategies to find the treasure in the fewest moves.

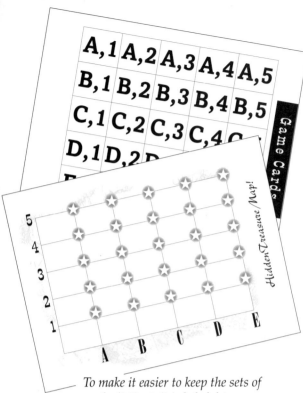

To make it easier to keep the sets of cards distinct, it is helpful to duplicate the cards onto at least four different colors of card stock. Then you will have four sets of cards in four different colors. If you have access to more colors, duplicate in as many colors as possible.

What You Need

For the class:
- ❏ 16 filled treasure boxes
- ❏ 16 sheets of 8 ½" x 11" colored card stock to make Game Cards (master on page 57)
- ❏ 16–32 pieces of 11" x 17" paper for the Hidden Treasure Map gameboard (master on page 92)
- ❏ 16 rubber bands
- ❏ 16 file folders
- ❏ 240 markers (lima beans, plastic disks, etc.)
- ❏ 16 small containers or ziplock plastic bags

Getting Ready

1. Duplicate the Game Cards (master on page 57) onto the colored card stock. You will need one set per pair of students. Cut each sheet along the lines to create the 25 individual cards that the students will need to play the game. Put a rubber band around each set of cards.

2. Duplicate the Hidden Treasure Map (master on page 92) onto the 11" x 17" paper to create the gameboards for this activity. Teachers of younger students or those who only want to do Session 1 will only need one map per pair of students. If your students will do both Session 1 and 2, duplicate one board per student in your class.

3. Put 15 markers into each small plastic container—such as a reused yogurt, cottage cheese, or margarine container. The markers will be used as a record keeping tool while playing the game in Session 2.

4. Choose treasure that will fit well on the map. You may want to let your students help decide which treasure boxes to use. For this activity, each pair of students needs any **25 pieces of treasure for Session 1** and **10 pieces for Session 2.**

5. Have materials on hand to demonstrate the games.

   a. When demonstrating **Session 1: Hidden Treasure Hunt,** gather the following: one Hidden Treasure Map gameboard, one set of Game Cards, and 25 pieces of treasure.

   b. When demonstrating **Session 2: Hidden Treasure Game,** gather the following: two Hidden Treasure Map gameboards, one file folder, 10 pieces of treasure, and one container with 15 markers.

Session 1: Hidden Treasure Hunt for Grades K–3

1. Gather the students in a group area and ask them if they have heard of treasure maps before. Ask what a treasure map is and who might use one.

2. Hold up a copy of the Hidden Treasure Map gameboard. Ask for observations about it. Focus attention on the large letters along the bottom of the map. As you point to each one, read it aloud with the students. Then point to the numbers and read them aloud **from bottom to top.** Point out the intersections of the lines which are marked by stars.

One teacher made an overhead of the Hidden Treasure Map gameboard and projected it on a classroom wall to introduce the coordinates. Another teacher made a giant treasure map grid on the playground with chalk. She had the students "walk" to the coordinates.

3. Ask where "A, 3" is on the map. Locate that point (marked by a star) by first reading across to the "A" and then counting up (above the "A") three stars. Continue with another set of coordinates, such as "C, 4."

4. Tell the students you are going to place treasure on all of the intersections/stars. Ask, "How many pieces of treasure are needed?" When a student replies, ask how they counted. Use this opportunity to count by fives.

5. Choose a student partner to hunt for treasures with you. Together place the 25 pieces of treasure on the map.

6. Tell students that there are cards that have a letter and a number on them to help find the treasure. Take a card from the top of the stack. Ask the students to read the coordinates. Find those coordinates by first reading across to the appropriate letter. Then count up until you reach the coordinates on the card. Take the treasure.

An alternate way of playing that some teachers have suggested is to lay out all the coordinate cards and have a child find the card she needs in order to take off the "treasure" he or she wants.

7. Now it is your partner's turn. Have her take a card and read the coordinates. Have her go first to the letter and then count up to the appropriate number. She then takes her treasure.

8. Continue to demonstrate for one more turn each or until you feel that your students are ready to play the game with a partner.

9. Send partners to their desks with a gameboard and a set of cards. Pass out a treasure box to partners and let the playing begin.

10. Circulate and observe how the students are using the coordinate grid and cooperating. Stress that this is a cooperative game. As time permits, allow partners to play the game more than one time.

11. Have partners clean up. Ask them to return the treasures to their boxes, put a rubber band around the cards, and return materials to designated locations.

Session 2: Hidden Treasure Game for Grades 1–3

1. Tell your students they are now going to play a more challenging version of the Hidden Treasure Map game. Explain that you are going to "hide" treasure on your map **without** them seeing where it is hidden. Then they are going to guess where the treasure is hidden.

2. Using a file folder as a screen, hide the Hidden Treasure Map gameboard from the students' view. Show the students the 10 pieces of treasure you are going to hide on different coordinates on the map. Hide the treasure.

3. Ask the students to guess where the treasure is hidden. Take guesses of coordinates, one at a time, until at least two treasures are found. Ask students how they are going to keep track of their guesses so they don't guess the same coordinate twice.

4. Tell students that when they play the game each person will get a Hidden Treasure Map gameboard. One partner will use it to hide treasure and the other partner will use it as a tool to record guesses.

5. Demonstrate how to play with a partner. Pick a partner and let her take over your spot with the gameboard behind

the file folder. Have her hide the 10 treasures on new coordinates. Use the other gameboard and the container with 15 markers for yourself.

6. Tell the rest of the class that they can help you guess where the treasures are hidden. When you guess your first set of coordinates, do one of the following.

a. If there is NO treasure on that location, place a marker on those coordinates on your gameboard.

b. If there IS a treasure, take it from your partner and place the treasure on those coordinates on your gameboard.

7. Continue to play so that students will catch on to the guessing and recording procedure. Have students help you with your guesses to keep them engaged. Play until all 10 treasures are found.

8. Send the partners to their desks with gameboards, file folders, and markers. Distribute treasures for students to hide.

9. Tell the partners to switch roles after each game. Circulate and observe them playing. You are likely to hear sounds of excitement during this game, especially when someone finds a treasure. This is fine—it reflects not only your students' enthusiasm, but also their success at using a coordinate grid.

10. At the end of the work period, ask students if they developed any special methods for finding the treasure. Ask about the number of guesses needed to find all the treasures. What was the smallest number of guesses? Have the students clean up the materials according to your directions.

11. Have the game available during other work periods for students to keep playing and trying new challenges (as in the "Going Further" section).

Going Further

1. New Versions of the Hunt and Game

a. You may want to modify the game for your students. You could come up with various changes. For example, in the Hidden Treasure Map Hunt, you could make duplicate cards for some coordinates. In this case, a player may not get a treasure on his turn since it will already have been found. Alternately, you could remove some of the cards, so that not all of the treasures are found.

b. For the Hidden Treasure Map Game, you may want to add more challenges! Players could be limited to only 15 guesses to see how many treasures they find.

c. Encourage your students to design their own versions of the game!

Turtle Math is available for Macintosh systems. For more information, contact Learning Services, P.O. Box 10636, Eugene, OR 97440-2636, (800) 877-9378. Ask for their teacher discount.

2. Computer Connection. Students have fun taking their "turtles" on a scavenger hunt using the program Turtle Math. This computer activity provides a wonderful way for students to practice LOGO programming. In addition, students practice counting by tens, distinguishing right from left, and using 90-degree angles as they find the treasures.

3. Create Maps to Special Spots. Begin by reading the book, *The Secret Birthday Message* by Eric Carle. In this story, a young boy gets a secret message on his birthday. After he follows the shapes that are used as clues to a series of destinations, he finds his birthday treasure! At the end of the story, a map of his complete path is revealed. This story, combined with the experience of treasure maps, can inspire students to create their own unique maps to destinations in and around the school.

In the GEMS Teacher's Guide, Group Solutions, *there is a section on maps that would go well with this activity.*

4. Local Maps. The book, *As the Crow Flies: A First Book of Maps* by Gail Hartman, can initiate another map project for older students. After reading the book, students can create a map of their neighborhood and place themselves in it. In addition, you could bring in maps of your local area to have students practice using its grid to locate various points of interest.

Game Cards

A,5	B,5	C,5	D,5	E,5
A,4	B,4	C,4	D,4	E,4
A,3	B,3	C,3	D,3	E,3
A,2	B,2	C,2	D,2	E,2
A,1	B,1	C,1	D,1	E,1

Activity 6: Sharing Treasures

Overview

In this activity, the students have many opportunities to divide up and share items of high interest. In Session 1, they share cereal to set the stage for sharing treasures fairly. This makes division come alive! At the end of the process, each person needs to understand how the cereal was divided and agree that it was divided fairly before anyone can eat even one piece. After all students have finished sharing and eating, their strategies for dividing the cereal are discussed.

In Session 2, the groups decide how to divide up a small collection of treasures—again, it should be done equitably. From their experiences with cereal sharing, students now have some strategies to draw on as they divide the treasures equally. Next, a class discussion of sharing strategies broadens their thinking on the different ways the division can be done. Following the discussion, each group puts their treasures back in one large pile. Then more treasures may be added to the original amount. This provides an opportunity for students to try a different method to fairly divide this new amount.

As students are busily sharing and dividing, they are working cooperatively, gaining a concrete understanding of division, building multiplication facts, using their estimation skills, and solving problems in many ways.

What You Need

For the class:
- ❏ 8–16 filled treasure boxes
- ❏ 8–16 clean paper cups, each large enough to hold ¼ cup of cereal
- ❏ 1 15 oz. box of Cheerios® **or** any other similar cereal with pieces of **uniform shape and size**
- ❏ 8–16 plastic containers
- ❏ a ¼ cup measuring cup
- ❏ 8–16 pieces of 12" x 18" construction paper
- ❏ 32 student journals **or** sheets of paper
- ❏ 32 pencils **or** pens
- ❏ chart paper
- ❏ 1 marker
- ❏ (*optional*) a copy of *The Doorbell Rang*

Getting Ready

1. Consider reading the story, *The Doorbell Rang*, as an opener to the sharing activities. If you plan to do so, obtain a copy of the book and familiarize yourself with it.

2. For kindergartners and first graders, we suggest that students continue to work in pairs for this final activity. We recommend that second and third graders be placed in groups of four. You know your students best, so decide on a way to group your students. Be consistent with both sessions—stick with either pairs or groups of four.

3. Purchase a box of cereal, such as Cheerios, that has pieces of uniform shape and size. **Just before presenting Session 1,** fill each of the paper cups with ¼ cup of the cereal. Place these cups in a spot that is easily accessible to students. Have chart paper and a marker available to record their methods for sharing cereal. Also have the construction paper available.

4. Decide which treasures your students will use for the sharing activity in Session 2. Select about 35 treasures for kindergarten and first grade students and about 50 treasures for second and third grade students. **Just before Session 2,** fill each of the plastic containers—such as reused yogurt, cottage cheese, or margarine containers—with treasures and set them aside. Have student journals or paper available for students to record their methods of dividing treasures. Also have the construction paper available.

The delightful story, The Doorbell Rang *by Pat Hutchins, provides an inviting introduction to "sharing" or division. See the "Literature Connections" section.*

One teacher wanted to use a more interesting cereal and chose Lucky Charms®—however, the different colors and shapes created major problems for sharing equitably and the students lost focus on the purpose of the activity. Another teacher used Lucky Charms successfully as a challenge for her third graders after first doing the sharing activity with Cheerios.

*The purpose of this activity is to keep the **focus on sharing the total number** of items rather than to worry about someone getting a larger or smaller shell (or other treasure item). The students will be more successful with the activity if you select items that are about the same size, such as keys, bread tags, bottle caps, buttons, beans, pasta, and stamps.*

Session 1: Cereal Sharing

1. If you've decided to begin the sharing activities with a story, read *The Doorbell Rang* to the class. Discuss how the children in the story shared the cookies each time the doorbell rang.

2. Tell your students that they are going to try to equally share something to eat. In this case, it is Cheerios which they *will* get to eat at the *end* of the activity.

3. Explain that each pair or group will receive a small cup of cereal that they are to pour onto a piece of construction paper. They are to share the small cupful of cereal any way that they choose, as long as after they have divided up the cereal each person:
   - has the same number of pieces,
   - understands how the cereal was divided, and
   - can explain the method used to divide the cereal equally.

You may want to write the rules for sharing on chart paper or the chalkboard so that students can refer back to them as they divide the cereal.

4. Tell students to raise their hands to have you check their work when they have finished the activity. They can eat their portions of cereal after they have successfully shared their methods with you.

5. Be sure students understand the directions. Pass out the cups of cereal and the construction paper to the partners or groups and let the sharing begin.

6. As students are busy dividing the cereal, circulate and watch their methods and strategies. Check their work and have each pair or group explain their method to you.

Don't be surprised if you observe or hear some unusual methods. In one class, a pair of students began by drawing rectangles. Next, they each put cereal around the perimeter of their rectangle. With the remaining cereal, they began to fill their rectangles. A problem occurred when one person had no more space to fill and the other person did. Finally, they began to count how many pieces of cereal they each had used.

7. When all your students have finished dividing and have eaten their cereal, conduct a class discussion on the various methods used to divide the cereal. Record these strategies on chart paper as each new one is explained. (Note: You will add new methods for sharing to this class list in Session 2.)

Session 2: Dividing Up Treasure!

1. Tell the students that they are going to do another sharing activity—this time using a cupful of treasures poured onto a piece of construction paper.

Reminder: To keep students focused on the division aspect of this activity, be sure to use treasure that is conducive to sharing equally.

Students have suggested such methods as weighing the treasures, using a number line, building towers of equal height, taking 1, 2, 5, etc. at a time, filling a cup to the same level, and tally marks. They have also suggested estimating amounts, then counting and equalizing quantities. See what additional methods your students come up with!

The book, Divide and Ride, *shows how the number 11 can be divided in many ways as a group of 11 best friends go on carnival rides with varying numbers of seats. See the "Literature Connections" section for this and other books related to division.*

2. Once again, the same guidelines for sharing apply. The treasures must be divided so that each person:
- has the same number of pieces,
- understands the method used, and
- can explain the method used.

When partners reach this point, let them know that they should raise their hands and explain their methods to you.

3. Review the list of methods that were used to share the cereal. Encourage the students to try a different method for sharing treasures than they used for cereal.

4. Distribute the containers of treasures and the construction paper to students. Encourage them to predict how many pieces of treasure they will each have when the treasures are divided equally.

5. Circulate and observe how the students are dividing the treasures.

6. When you have observed that most partners or groups have divided their treasures at least one way, use your usual signal to get your students' attention. Have a class discussion on their methods for sharing the treasures. Record any new methods on the class list started in Session 1.

7. After this discussion, encourage the students to gather their collection of treasures back into one group to divide it again using another method. Ask if they think they will get the same results. Alternately, you may want to add more treasure items before they divide it again. Have them predict how many treasures they will have this time.

8. Have student record one method of dividing the treasures in their journals or on paper. This helps students to articulate one process for division.

9. Ask which methods they think work best for dividing things. Have students explain their thinking when they respond. If your students are ready for a further discussion, pose another question. Ask which method they think is best for dividing a set number of treasures among four people. Why? Have them explain their thinking.

Going Further

1. Sharing Classroom Materials. Ask what other items they could share in the classroom. Create a list of appropriate items. This list may include crayons, unifix cubes, pencil erasers, and toothpicks. Let students choose a group of items to practice dividing fairly either in pairs or groups of four.

2. Sharing Other Food Items. On another day, challenge each pair or group of four to divide a single, divisible item, such as a banana, among themselves. This is a good introduction to fractional parts. Another item to share that has lots of unequal pieces is a small, individual-size bag of potato chips. See how they divide these items among themselves. Your students may want to bring in other items for sharing.

3. Bean Division Challenge (for second and third graders only). Give pairs or groups of four students a handful of beans. Ask them to predict how many each person will get and then divide them fairly. After this first division, have the students push the beans back into the middle of the table. Walk around to each pair or group and add a small amount of beans. Again, have students predict how many beans each person will get, taking into account the extra beans added. Then they divide the beans again, but this time they must *use a different method* than the one they used the first time. If time permits and students are able, do a third division. For this third division, walk around to each group and remove some beans from the pile. Again, have students predict how many beans each person will get and *use a different method* than they have used for the other two bean divisions.

The book, A Remainder of One, *is a wonderful way to introduce the bean sharing activity. Another book by the same author,* One Hundred Hungry Ants, *is a great introduction to division without remainders. See the "Literature Connections" section.*

Going Further (for the entire unit)

1. Living Treasures. Take the idea of treasures to a higher level. In Japan and other countries, there are esteemed artisans who are designated "Living Treasures." Some include master potters, carpenters, and painters. Discuss this concept. Think about museums that house treasures both ancient and modern. Consider the natural world and the treasures that abound there. Make a class book of living treasures. The treasures can include plants, animals, or people. Have students think about a valuable living treasure. Draw a picture and explain why that person, animal, or plant is a treasure.

2. "Hidden" Treasure in Cupcakes. To go along with all the fun and excitement of treasures, especially with the treasure hunt in Activity 5, the opportunity to share this wonderful idea could not be missed. It is not for everyone, but it is a winner with kids and adults alike. Collect enough small metal charms so that there will be one for each student in the class. Wrap each charm in aluminum foil or parchment paper. Make a recipe of cake batter to use for cupcakes. After you have filled the cups with batter, place one wrapped charm into each uncooked "cupcake." Bake according to directions. When you pass out the cupcakes, tell the students to eat them carefully because there are treasures hidden within the cupcakes. You can either let each student keep the treasure in his cupcake or collect them and create a new treasure box of charms for your class. Perhaps take a class vote to decide. It would be interesting to see what the students choose to do.

In connection with the coordinate mapping activities in Activity 5, one teacher reported hiding treasures in a sheet cake and decorating the top to match the Hidden Treasure Map gameboard. In turn, each student took a game card with coordinates and then had the fun of digging up a treasure at those coordinates!

3. 100th Day of School Collections. Encourage students to bring in collections of 100 objects on the 100th Day of School. You may want to suggest that the objects have a "theme" or be related in some way. Review the types of treasure boxes you have to spark and inspire ideas for new ones. When the collections come in, have students organize them in different ways. Just as they did with treasures, they can sort and graph the collections. They can also do activities related to number and place value. For example, they can organize their collections in groups of 10. You may want to challenge older students to see how they can divide the 100 objects to create equal groups—similar to Activity 6. For younger students, assist them by asking how many groups of five (or two, four, 20, 25, 50) objects there are in 100.

4. Treasure NIM. Use treasure items to play a variety of logic games based on the ancient Chinese game of NIM. In each version of the game, students use logical-thinking and problem-solving skills. A good version to start with uses 10 pieces of treasure and has two players. The object of the game is to be the player who takes the last piece of treasure from the trove that the game starts with. For example:

- Start with 10 pieces of treasure.
- Each player can take either one or two pieces of treasure at a time.
- As long as there is treasure, a player must take some.
- The player who takes the last piece of treasure wins. The last piece can be taken as one of the last two pieces.

After students master this version, switch to 12 pieces of treasure. How does the strategy change when the game is altered in this way? Continue to vary the game. Increase to 15 pieces of treasure and this time players can take one, two, or three pieces of treasure. Older students can be challenged to use 20 pieces of treasure. At some point, you may want to also change the object of the game such that you *do not* want to take the last piece of treasure—a "Polite Pirate" version of the game!

5. Make A Treasure Box! During the creation of your treasure boxes or along the path of the activities in this guide, you may want to set aside time for your students to make their own special treasure boxes. They can be fashioned out of recycled materials—such as shoe boxes or candy boxes—or be crafted out of new materials. Some students used treasure items to decorate the outside of their boxes. Let your students' creativity run free as they design and create.

6. Estimating Treasures. Your treasures are a wonderful source of items to fill an estimation jar. Choose a plastic jar that holds a number of items that are appropriate for your students. Fill the jar with treasures from one box. Be sure the treasures are relatively uniform in size—for example, bread tags or keys. Put the jar in a place where students have access to it along with just one item like those on the inside. This gives students a point of reference to estimate how many total items are in the jar. When it is time to determine how many are in the jar, either have the class count together with the assistance of a place value board, or have a pair of students determine the number. Record the number. During the following weeks, fill the *same* jar

with another treasure item. Keep a list of the number of each item that fit in the jar. How does this list help as they make new estimations? Another variation is to use the same treasure item and change the size of the jar that you fill!

See the "Frog Guesstimation" activity in the GEMS Teacher's Guide, Frog Math: Predict, Ponder, Play, *for more information on estimation.*

Sources for Materials

Boxes for Treasures

Arvey Paper and Office Products

The business card boxes from this office supply company are strongly recommended for treasures because they are sturdy, come assembled, and do not need to be covered with contact paper. The boxes come in several sizes; listed are two that work best for small treasures. There are Arvey stores located throughout the United States. The toll-free number listed below can provide you with the retail store closest to you and can also be used to order.

(800) 600-0064 for the location of retail stores or to order directly

Business Card Boxes #14809
10 $\frac{1}{16}$" x 3 $\frac{5}{8}$" x 2"
30¢ each or $58/case of 200 boxes

Business Card Boxes #14808
7 $\frac{1}{8}$" x 3 $\frac{5}{8}$" x 2"
25¢ each or $48/case of 200 boxes

Treasure Items
The following sources carry shells, plastic animals, trinkets, and other treasure items.

Concepts To Go
P.O. Box 10043
Berkeley, CA 94709
(510) 848-3233
fax (510) 486-1248

Creative Publications
5623 West 115th Street
Worth, IL 60482–9931
(800) 624-0822
fax (800) 624-0821

Lakeshore Learning Materials
2695 E. Dominguez Street
P. O. Box 6261
Carson, CA 90749
(800) 421-5354

Nasco Arts and Crafts
901 Janesville Avenue
Ft. Atkinson, WI 53538-0901
(414) 563-2446 or (800) 558-9595
fax (414) 563-8296
http://www.nascofa.com

4825 Stoddard Road
Modesto, CA 95356-9318
(209) 545-1600
fax (209) 545-1669

U. S. Toy Company Inc.
1227 East 119th Street
Grandview, MO 64030
(800) 255-6124

Assessment Suggestions

Selected Student Outcomes

1. Students improve in their ability to observe, identify, describe, and compare attributes of various objects.

2. Students are able to sort, classify, and graph objects according to their attributes. Older students organize their sorts using a Venn diagram.

3. Students can record and interpret observations of their sorts and graphs.

4. Students become more skillful at using a coordinate grid.

5. Students are able to use logical thinking skills to develop and describe strategies they use to solve problems.

6. Students improve in their ability to apply number sense as they interpret data and do informal division.

Built-in Assessment Activities

Treasures. In Activity 2: Exploring Treasures, pairs of students explore the treasures they collected, including bottle caps, stamps, and buttons. They share and record their observations of the similarities and differences of the items. The teacher notes the language used to describe the attributes of the treasures, and how students verbally and in writing communicate their observations. (Outcomes 1, 2)

Sorts and Graphs. In Activity 3: Treasures of Many Sorts and Activity 4: Treasure Graphs, students continue to explore their treasures and identify specific attributes, including color, shape, size, and texture. Next, students sort and graph the items to organize groups by attributes. Older students are introduced to the Venn diagram as another way to organize their treasures. The teacher uses their responses to gain feedback on their understanding of the sorting and graphing process and their number sense. (Outcomes 1, 2, 3, 6)

Finding Hidden Treasure. In Activity 5: Treasure Maps, students play board games where they must find treasure "hidden" on a coordinate grid. When the game is changed to make finding the treasures more difficult, students develop problem solving skills as they come up with strategies to accurately find the treasure. During these activities, the teacher observes the students using the coordinate grid and listens for language that describes their strategies and explanations for finding the treasures. (Outcomes 4, 5)

Share It Fair. In Activity 6: Sharing Treasures, a team of four students begins by dividing fairly a handful of cereal and then continues by dividing a collection of treasures. As students design and conduct their sharing process, the teacher observes the process and makes note of the strategies that emerge and how they are carried out and communicated. In addition, when the students report on how they shared the treasures, the teacher gains insight into their number sense. (Outcomes 5, 6)

Additional Assessment Ideas

Treasure Book. Have students pretend they are sending a book about treasures to the inhabitants on the planet Venus. Have them write or dictate a detailed description explaining their favorite treasure item. They can include a picture to enhance their descriptions. Their descriptions can be put together in a class Treasure Book. (Outcomes 1, 2)

Treasure Chest! Give students a box containing a mixture of treasures from all of the treasure boxes. Have them come up with several different ways to sort the treasures and to record one of the sorts. (Outcomes 1, 2, 3)

More Treasure Boxes. Encourage students to find another treasure item to collect and create a treasure box to explore, sort, and graph. Have students record one of the graphs and pose three questions that could be answered by looking at the graph. (Outcomes 1, 2, 3)

Treasure Games. Challenge students to design other strategy games using the treasures they have collected. (Outcomes 1, 5)

Fair Shares. Give groups of four students (or pairs of students) a collection of 12 items. Have them determine how many ways the 12 items can be divided fairly (2 groups of 6; 3 groups of 4; 4 groups of 3; 6 groups of 2; 12 groups of 1). Alternately give students a collection of 25 items to determine how many people are needed to divide the items equally. How can 50 items be divided? (Outcomes 5, 6)

Bottle Caps!!

1. there were 4 golden one's, 2. there were 2 bron one's, 3. there were 2 one's whith their tag still on 4. there were 5 one's whith ckind-of Chineys Diseny one's, 5. there were 10 speshle fancy ons, 6. there were 4 sona one's, 7. there were 2 cool one's 8. there were 14. plain evry-day one's.

THE

Literature Connections

Alligator Shoes
by Arthur Dorros
E. P. Dutton, New York. 1982
Grades: Preschool–2

When an alligator accidentally becomes locked in a shoe store overnight, he spends his time trying on a variety of shoes. As he puts on each type the illustration shows him in the setting appropriate for each shoe. This is a good book to introduce sorting, especially for younger students.

Anthony Ant's Treasure Hunt
by Lorna and Graham Philpot
Random House, New York. 1996
Grades: K–3

When Anthony finds a treasure map under his bedroom floor, he begins an exciting journey to find a long-lost cache of jewels. The treasure map leads Anthony (and the reader!) through a maze with clues on each page. Flaps to lift and a fold-out maze/map make the book interactive. A great connection to Activity 5.

As the Crow Flies: A First Book of Maps
by Gail Hartman; illustrated by Harvey Stevenson
Bradbury Press, New York. 1991
Grades: Preschool–2

This book provides a look at different geographical areas from the perspectives of an eagle, rabbit, crow, horse, and gull. There is a verbal account of each animal's journey followed by an overhead view of the animal's path. The last page includes a big map, a larger context into which each of the smaller maps fits. It is an excellent book to introduce or reinforce mapping skills.

Aunt Ippy's Museum of Junk
by Rodney A. Greenblat
HarperCollins, New York. 1991
Grades: K–2

A brother and sister visit their ecology-minded Aunt Ippy and her world-famous Museum of Junk, which includes treasures such as a barrel of one-of-a-kind shoes and a sack of clocks. This story can inspire a class to begin a collection of treasure boxes, to raise awareness of recycling and

There are "countless" great books that make strong literature connections to Treasure Boxes. *Since this guide was first published, GEMS has received numerous suggestions from teachers, including:*
A String of Beads *by Margarette S. Reid, Dutton Books, 1977.*
Amelia's Road *by Linda Jacobs Altman, Lee and Low Books, New York, 1993.*
17 Kings and 42 Elephants *by Margaret Mahy, E.P. Dutton, 1987 (for Activity 6).*
Sweet Magnolia *by Virginia Kroll, Charlesbridge Publishing, 1995.*
Pirates: Robbers of the High Seas *by Gail Gibbons, Scholastic, Inc., 1993 (for Treasure Maps).*

reusing materials in new and different ways. Such a collection also provides new math manipulatives for teaching many concepts, including sorting and classifying.

The Best Vacation Ever
by Stuart J. Murphy; illustrated by Nadine Bernard Westcott
HarperCollins, New York. 1997
Grades: 1–4

In this book, which introduces survey graphs in a meaningful context, a young girl decides that her busy family needs a vacation. To help determine what vacation would meet all their needs, she surveys her family and then analyzes her data only to discover that the best vacation ever is in their own backyard!

The Button Box
by Margarette S. Reid; illustrated by Sarah Chamberlain
Dutton Children's Books, New York. 1990
Grades: Preschool–2

This book is a wonderful introduction to sorting buttons. A young boy explores his grandmother's button box and categorizes buttons by various attributes. Reading this story is likely to inspire students to sort buttons many ways!

Caps for Sale
by Esphyr Slobodkina
W. R. Scott, New York. 1947
Harper & Row, New York. 1985
Grades: Preschool–4

When a peddler takes a nap under a tree, a band of mischievous monkeys steal all the caps he has neatly stacked on his head. This classic story is useful with counting, sorting, or graphing activities.

Divide and Ride
by Stuart J. Murphy; illustrated by George Ulrich
HarperCollins, New York. 1997
Grades: 2–5

This book provides a great introduction to or review of division. It shows how the number 11 can be divided in many ways as a group of 11 best friends go on carnival rides with varying numbers of seats.

The Doorbell Rang
by Pat Hutchins
Greenwillow Books, New York. 1986
Grades: Preschool–4

This delightful story provides an inviting introduction to
"sharing" or division. Each time the doorbell rings, there
are more people who arrive and share the dozen delicious
cookies that Ma made! But when twelve hungry children
are already seated at the table and the doorbell rings again,
who can figure out how everyone will get a fair share?
This well-known, and well-loved, book is a wonderful
opener to the sharing activities.

Everybody Needs a Rock
by Byrd Baylor; illustrated by Peter Parnall
Scribner, New York. 1974
Grades: K–5

This book describes the qualities to consider when select-
ing the perfect rock for play and pleasure. In so doing, the
properties of color, size, shape, texture, and smell are
discussed in such a way that you'll want to rush out and
find a rock of your own. Provides a nice introduction to
attributes of rocks.

Gator Pie
by Louise Mathews; illustrated by Jeni Bassett
Dodd, Mead, New York. 1979
Grades: 2–5

Two young alligators find a pie near the edge of a swamp
and decide to share it. As other alligators emerge from the
swamp and demand part of the pie, the portion for each
alligator gets smaller. This is a useful book for introducing
sharing and division.

The Greatest Treasure
by Arcadio Lobato
Picture Book Studio, Saxonville, Massachusetts. 1987
Grades: K–4

The time has come for the witches to choose a new queen.
The current queen will award this honor to the witch who
finds the most special treasure. The most valuable treasure
is one that no money can buy—friendship! Delightfully
illustrated in watercolors by the Spanish author-illustrator.
Useful in Activity 1 for conveying that many things can be
treasures.

The **I Spy** series of books
by Walter Wick and Jean Marzollo
Scholastic, New York. 1992–1996
Grades: K–5

Each thematic book in this series contains photographs
with incredible collections of objects—many that could
come from a treasure box! Each two-page spread is accompanied by rhyming verses that ask the reader to find
objects hidden in the photographs. Young and old students alike hone their observation skills as they comb each
page. Many more questions or riddles could be posed to
further delve into the attributes of the objects in the photographs. The titles in the series include *I Spy* (1992), *I Spy
Christmas* (1992), *I Spy Fun House* (1993), *I Spy Mystery*
(1993), *I Spy Fantasy* (1994), *I Spy School Days* (1995), and *I
Spy Spooky Night* (1996).

The Keeping Quilt
by Patricia Polacco
Simon & Schuster, New York. 1988
Grades: Preschool–3

A homemade quilt ties together the lives of four generations of an immigrant Jewish family. Made from their old
clothes, it helps them remember back home "like having
the family in Russia dance around us at night." The quilt,
a cherished family treasure, is used in marriage ceremonies, as a tablecloth, and as a blanket for a newborn child.

Maps and Mapping
by Barbara Taylor
Kingfisher Books, New York. 1993
Grades: 2–4

Through clear illustrations and inviting text, this book
explains what maps are and why they are used, introduces
symbols found on maps, and describes how cartographers
map the world. It includes related activities for the reader
to develop a deeper understanding of maps. Ties in
strongly with Activity 5.

On My Beach There Are Many Pebbles
by Leo Lionni
Obolensky, New York. 1961
Grades: Preschool–3

This book invites the reader to take a closer look at the many types of pebbles that can be found on a beach. Though there are many "ordinary" pebbles, by looking at them carefully and with a bit of imagination, they can take on new qualities. For example, they are grouped into "fishpebbles" and "numberpebbles." Provides a great springboard into sorting and classifying rocks and pebbles.

One Hundred Hungry Ants
by Elinor J. Pinczes; illustrated by Bonnie MacKain
Houghton Mifflin, Boston. 1993
Grades: Preschool–3

Told in lilting rhyme, this is the playful story of an ant colony swarming toward a picnic. As they march along, the littlest ant stops the procession and suggests they divide into different line formations to arrive at the picnic more quickly. In the end, however, the ants' rearrangements cause them to miss out on all the food! This book makes a great math connection as an early introduction to the principles of division without remainders. It's also useful in teaching the real-world activity of how to make change for a dollar. All ages will love to follow along with the actions of these happy, but hungry, ants.

A Remainder of One
by Elinor J. Pinczes; illustrated by Bonnie MacKain
Houghton Mifflin, Boston. 1995
Grades: Preschool–3

When the 25th squadron of bugs march past their queen, she is dismayed to see that the lines of bugs are uneven. One bug, Joe by name, is left behind—a remainder of one. Knowing that their queen does not like untidy lines, the bugs divide themselves into different lines. It is only after several tries that Joe is included in *even* lines that march by the queen to the delight of all. Colorful and playful illustrations abound in this fun book that introduces the concept of division and remainders.

Roxaboxen
by Alice McLerran; illustrated by Barbara Cooney
Lothrop, Lee & Shepard, New York. 1991
Grades: K–4

From a hill covered with sand, rocks, old wooden boxes and thorny plants, Marian, her sisters and friends create an imaginary town called Roxaboxen. The round black pebbles that they find there are thought of as buried treasure and become the money of Roxaboxen. This book, based on the experience of the author, celebrates the wonders of creative imagination.

The Secret Birthday Message
by Eric Carle
Crowell, New York. 1972
Grades: Preschool–2

In this story, a young boy gets a secret message on his birthday. After he follows the shapes that are used as clues to a series of destinations, he finds his birthday treasure! At the end of the story, a map of his complete path is revealed. This story, combined with the experience of treasure maps, can inspire students to create their own unique maps to destinations in and around the school.

Shoes
by Elizabeth Winthrop; illustrated by William Joyce
Harper & Row, New York. 1986
Grades: Preschool–2

Delightful illustrations show a group of children wearing many types of shoes and participating in a variety of activities as rhyming text describes it all. This survey of shoes concludes that the best of all are the perfect natural "shoes" that are your feet. Great to read before doing a survey of shoes or sorting and classifying real shoes.

Shoes, Shoes, Shoes
by Ann Morris; photographs by Ken Heyman
Lothrop, Lee & Shepard, New York. 1995
Grades: Preschool–3

Photos and simple text describe all kinds of shoes—some
for dancing, walking, playing, some for snow or ice, some
made of wood or cloth. A great book to kick off sorting
and graphing activities. Several other books by this au-
thor/photographer team are also recommended, including
Hats, Hats, Hats (Lothrop, Lee & Shepard, 1989), *Bread,
Bread, Bread* (Lothrop, Lee & Shepard, 1989), *Loving*
(Lothrop, Lee & Shepard, 1990), *Tools* (Lothrop, Lee &
Shepard, 1992), and *Houses and Homes* (Lothrop, Lee &
Shepard, 1992).

**A Taste of the Mexican Market/El Gusto del Mercado
Mexicano**
by Nancy María Grande Tabor
Charlesbridge, Watertown, Massachusetts. 1996
Grades: Preschool–3

The reader is taken on a visit to a Mexican market and
encounters a wide array of food—including beans, a
possible treasure box item, and other household items.
Each display of food is rich in diversity and many questions are posed that focus on the attributes of the various
items. Other questions relate to math concepts such as
measurement (weight of vegetables) and statistics (survey
of favorite fruit bar).

A Three Hat Day
by Laura Geringer; illustrated by Arnold Lobel
Harper & Row, New York. 1985
Grades: Preschool–3

R. R. Pottle loves hats and has a rather large and varied
collection. However, he is lonely. To cheer himself up one
day he puts on three of his favorite hats and goes for a
walk. As he walks along he sees others in couples and this
makes him more lonely. So he decides to go to the largest
hat store in town. Upon seeing all the beautiful hats his
spirits begin to soar. Then he sees the woman of his
dreams—and she's wearing the perfect hat. A helpful book
to introduce a hat sorting or graphing activity.

The Treasure
by Uri Shulevitz
Farrar, Straus, Giroux, New York. 1978
Grades: 1–5

In this interpretation of a familiar story, a poor man follows his recurring dream and journeys to a distant city in search of a treasure. Once there he is advised to return home to find it—which indeed he does, reminding us that "sometimes one must travel far to discover what is near."

The Way to Captain Yankee's
by Anne Rockwell
Macmillan, New York. 1994
Grades: Preschool–2

Miss Calico travels to see her friend Captain Yankee by following her carefully drawn map. Each part of her route is documented and the reader can follow along on a two-page map. Readers can even see where Miss Calico misses her turn and gets a bit lost. For preschoolers and kindergartners, this book provides a great introduction to maps.

Whose Shoes Are These?
by Ron Roy; photographs by Rosemarie Hausherr
Clarion Books, New York. 1988
Grades: Preschool–4

Text and photographs describe the appearance and function of almost twenty types of shoes, including work boots, snowshoes, and basketball sneakers. The question and answer layout of the book makes it interactive. A useful book to introduce sorting and graphing.

Summary Outlines

Activity 1: Collecting Treasures

Session 1: Setting the Stage to Collect Treasures

1. Introduce the unit. Ask students what a treasure means to them. Confirm responses related to material value, but add that a treasure can be something with special meaning. Share one of your own treasures. Say that treasures can be small interesting objects of many kinds and provide some examples, such as buttons, shells, rocks, etc.
2. Hold up a treasure box to help students visualize size of items. Start a list of items they might collect. Show them one of the construction paper squares. Have them each hold a paper square. Ask for other items about that size and add to list. Show how to use paper square to measure several objects of various sizes.
3. Tell students to bring in items from home for the class treasure boxes. These will not be returned. Emphasize that there is no need to BUY these, and that they can be recycled items, such as canceled stamps, bottle caps, bread tags, etc.
4. Give a letter home to each student, with paper square.
5. Encourage students to bring in items. They will start putting their treasures into boxes in one week. Have large box to store treasures.

Session 2: Filling the Boxes with Treasures

1. Have students take their treasures from the large box and sit in a circle. Distribute extra treasures as needed. Tell students this is the day to fill the treasure boxes. Add new items to the list.
2. Reread list, asking for raised hands if students brought an item. If several hands go up, label a box. If only one hand, wait until completing the list before labeling a box. (Don't label a box unless there are at least 10 items. More boxes can be created later.)
3. Place labeled boxes in center of circle. Ask students to guess which boxes they think will have the most treasures.
4. Have a student choose a labeled box and walk around circle to collect treasures, then continue the same process until all labeled boxes are filled.
5. Place remaining items in center. Can these be placed in a new box or boxes or existing ones? Decide as a class how to solve this problem.
6. Do some estimating. Ask which box has the most and least treasures. Explain that students can keep bringing in items.

7. Say that now the treasures belong to the whole class, not individual students.

Activity 2: Exploring Treasures

1. Encourage students to explore.
2. Discuss basic ground rules for working together.
3. Distribute treasure boxes and allow time for exploration.
4. Circulate, encouraging closer observation by asking questions.
5. After about 15–20 minutes, ask students to share their discoveries. Encourage discussion by asking questions.
6. Invite students to circulate, looking at, but not touching, the treasures being explored.
7. Give examples of recording discoveries and have students record.
8. Have students return treasures to the boxes.
9. Ask students to read or tell you about what the wrote.
10. Keep boxes available for more exploring during free choice times.

Activity 3: Treasures of Many Sorts

Session 1: Shoe Sort

1. Tell students they are going to sort their shoes. Have them remove one shoe, examine it, share observations with a neighbor, then place shoe in front of them.
2. Ask students to describe shoes, define attributes, and record them.
3. Say you want to sort shoes by one attribute, such as type of closure.
4. Encourage students to predict which group will have most and fewest. Sort shoes one by one with students placing them in appropriate group.
5. Ask questions to encourage mathematical observations.
6. Refer to list of attributes and record new ideas of ways to sort shoes.

Session 2: Sorting Treasures

1. Pour contents of a treasure box onto construction paper for visibility. Ask for some attributes.
2. Explain that you will sort the treasure by one attribute, such as color. Ask them to name colors of items. As they do, select one item of that color to "label" each color group. Then sort all the treasures.
3. Ask questions to encourage mathematical observations. Have a student review how the treasure was sorted. Then

push all of the items back together. Ask for and record other ways the treasure could be sorted.

4. Say that students will now sort a treasure box with a partner, with an already listed attribute or a new one. When finished, they should raise their hands.

5. Allow time for pairs to discuss attributes and sort. Circulate to observe and ask questions.

6. When pairs have finished ask, "How did you sort your treasures?" Encourage full explanations and discussion. Record any new ways to sort.

7. Have partners sort treasures in another way. Following this, have students circulate to see other sorts.

8. Have students write down one way they sorted. Ask for any new attributes and add to the list.

Session 3: Venn Diagrams to Sort Treasure (Grades 2–3)

1. Explain that you are going to sort in a new way and ask for descriptions (attributes) of the treasure you selected, such as buttons.

2. Say you are going to use yarn loops to sort the buttons. Label one circle "Round," and the other "Small."

3. Place buttons into the appropriate loop in this order: large, round; small, non-round; then a few more buttons that only fit into one of the circles.

4. Hold up a button that is both round and small. After student responses, pull the loops to create an overlapping area and label it "Round and Small." Place the button.

5. Continue placing buttons. If a button does not fit into any group, ask students for ideas; place button outside loops. Continue until at least 20 buttons have been placed.

6. Explain that you used a Venn diagram to organize the buttons. It is a tool for organizing information. Ask students what this Venn diagram communicates and to explain their thinking.

7. Students will work in partners to sort buttons using a Venn diagram.

8. List their ideas for two distinct groups that will also overlap, such as a color and shape, or a color and a size. You may also want to ask for their ideas on attributes that would not overlap.

9. Have students sort using buttons and loops. Circulate, asking them to explain their Venn diagrams. After groups finish, invite them to look at others.

10. Ask if Venn diagrams helped determine how the treasures were sorted or made it harder. Allow time for students to record their diagrams.

11. Challenge pairs of students to create an intersecting Venn diagram with another treasure item. Review the class list of attributes and ask for other ideas.

12. Distribute a treasure box and yarn loops to each pair and have them begin. When finished, have them "tour" the class. Challenge them to determine how treasures were sorted in each diagram.

13. Ask for comments and additional ideas for the class list. Provide time for students to record their diagrams.

14. With third grade students, after several Venn experiences, challenge them with questions about the information Venn diagrams provide. Pose questions to encourage mathematical and logical thinking.

Activity 4: Treasure Graphs

Session 1: Graphing Shoes

1. Have students remove one shoe and place it in front of themselves. Have them recall how they sorted shoes before and ask for additional ways to sort.

2. Place graphing grid on floor. Explain that this tool will be used to help organize their shoes into groups by an attribute. Decide on an attribute, such as type of closure.

3. Using shoes of different type, "label" each row. Have students predict which groups might have most and fewest. One by one have students place shoes in the proper row.

4. When all the shoes are on the graph, ask questions to elicit numerical and other mathematical observations.

Session 2: Graphing Treasures

1. Using bread tags or another visible treasure item, pour about 30 items onto construction paper.

2. Explain that you are going to organize the bread tags using a similar graphing grid that is smaller.

3. Hold up the small graphing grid and ask how it is similar and different from the large grid. Tell students you will graph the bread tags by color. "Label" each row with a different color bread tag.

4. With student volunteers, place the bread tags on the small graph. Ask for predictions as you go along.

5. When all bread tags are placed, ask for observations and true statements. If the class needs another example, repeat the demonstration with another attribute.

6. Give a treasure box to each pair of students and a small grid. They should take about 30 pieces and discuss attributes, then agree on one attribute to graph. When done, they should raise their hands for you to look at their graphs.

7. Encourage students to graph again, using a new attribute. Have them circulate around the room. As appro-

priate, have students record data on a pictorial or abstract graph, depending on age and experience.

Activity 5: Treasure Maps

Session 1: Hidden Treasure Hunt (Grades K–3)

1. Ask students about treasure maps.
2. Hold up the Hidden Treasure Hunt gameboard and ask for observations. Focus attention first on letters, reading aloud with class, then on numbers, reading aloud **from bottom to top**. Point out the intersections, marked by stars.
3. Ask where "A, 3" is. Locate it from letter to number, then do same with another set of coordinates.
4. Say you will place a treasure on all intersections. How many treasures are needed?
5. With a student, place 25 treasures on the map. Say there are cards with a letter and a number on them. Take a card and find that treasure. Then have your partner take a card and find a treasure. Continue until all students understand.
6. Give a gameboard and set of cards to pairs of students. Pass out a treasure box to each pair and have them begin.
7. Circulate, stressing that this is a cooperative game. If time permits, they can play more than one game.
8. Have partners return treasures to boxes, put a rubber band around cards, and return the materials.

Session 2: Hidden Treasure Game (Grades 1–3)

1. Introduce a more challenging version of the game. Treasure is hidden by one partner, without the other partner seeing where it is placed.
2. Using a file folder as screen, hide the gameboard. Show students the 10 pieces of treasure you will hide, then hide them on the map.
3. Ask for guesses. Take guesses of coordinates until two are found. Ask students how they could keep track of their guesses.
4. Explain that both partners will get a gameboard. One will use her board to hide the treasures; the other will use his board to record guesses. Demonstrate how to do this with yourself as the person who guesses. The class can help you. If there is no treasure on the coordinates guessed, place a marker there. If there is a treasure, have your partner give you that treasure and place it on your gameboard. Play until all 10 treasures are found.
5. When students understand the game, have partners begin. Have them switch roles after each game.

6. Near the end of the session, ask if students developed any special methods for finding the treasure. What was the smallest number of guesses needed?

7. Have student clean up the game and return materials. Have it available for later play. Challenge students to find the treasure in fewer than 15 guesses.

Activity 6: Sharing Treasures

Session 1: Cereal Sharing

1. If you wish, read *The Doorbell Rang* to the class. Discuss how children in the story shared cookies.

2. Say that students will be sharing an edible item, Cheerios, which they will get to eat at the END of the activity, not before!

3. Each pair (or group) receives a small cup of cereal that they pour onto a piece of construction paper. They can share as they wish, provided that each person has same number of pieces, understands how it was divided, and can explain the method used to divide it equally.

4. Have students raise their hands as they complete the sharing so you can check their work. After they have shared their methods with you, they can eat their portions of the cereal.

5. Circulate as students work and discuss methods with all groups as they finish.

6. Have a class discussion on the methods used. Record these strategies to start a list that will be added to in the next session.

Session 2: Dividing Up Treasure!

1. Introduce another sharing activity—this time with a cupful of treasures. The same guidelines apply (each person should have the same number of treasure pieces, all should understand how it was divided and be able to explain the method used). They should raise their hands when they complete their work.

2. Review list of methods used with cereal. Encourage partners (or groups) to try a different method than they used before.

3. Distribute treasures and construction paper and encourage students to predict how many treasures each will have after treasures are equally divided.

4. After most have divided their treasures at least one way, discuss methods used and add new methods to the list.

5. Have students gather their treasures together and divide them again, using another method. Will they get the same

results? (You may want to add more treasures before they try it again—if so, have them predict how many each will have this time.)

6. Ask which method they think worked best. Encourage them to record one of the methods they used.